Vue.js Quick Start Guide

Learn how to build amazing and complex reactive web
applications easily using Vue.js

Ajdin Imsirovic

BIRMINGHAM - MUMBAI

Vue.js Quick Start Guide

Commissioning Editor: Kunal Chaudari
Acquisition Editor: Siddharth Mandal
Content Development Editor: Kirk Dsouza
Technical Editor: Sushmeeta Jena
Copy Editor: Safis Editing
Project Coordinator: Hardik Bhinde
Proofreader: Safis Editing
Indexer: Rekha Nair
Graphics: Alishon Mendonsa
Production Coordinator: Nilesh Mohite

First published: October 2018

Production reference: 2091118

Published by Packt Publishing Ltd.
Livery Place
35 Livery Street
Birmingham
B3 2PB, UK.

ISBN 978-1-78934-410-3

www.packtpub.com

`mapt.io`

Mapt is an online digital library that gives you full access to over 5,000 books and videos, as well as industry leading tools to help you plan your personal development and advance your career. For more information, please visit our website.

Why subscribe?

- Spend less time learning and more time coding with practical eBooks and Videos from over 4,000 industry professionals

- Improve your learning with Skill Plans built especially for you

- Get a free eBook or video every month

- Mapt is fully searchable

- Copy and paste, print, and bookmark content

Packt.com

Did you know that Packt offers eBook versions of every book published, with PDF and ePub files available? You can upgrade to the eBook version at `www.packt.com` and as a print book customer, you are entitled to a discount on the eBook copy. Get in touch with us at `customercare@packtpub.com` for more details.

At `www.packt.com`, you can also read a collection of free technical articles, sign up for a range of free newsletters, and receive exclusive discounts and offers on Packt books and eBooks.

Contributors

About the author

Ajdin Imsirovic has been working with frontend technologies, as well as web and print design, for almost two decades. He is an accomplished video course creator and the author of *Bootstrap 4 Cookbook* and *Elm Web Development*, both by Packt Publishing. In his third book, *Vue.js Quick Start Guide*, he eases in the newcomers to the Vue ecosystem in a clear and concise manner.

> *I would like to thank my parents for raising me to understand and appreciate the value of hard work and the value of not giving up.*

About the reviewers

Sufyan bin Uzayr is a writer, teacher, and developer with more than 10 years' experience in the industry. He is an open source enthusiast and specializes in a wide variety of technologies. He holds four masters' degrees and has authored multiple books.

Sufyan is an avid writer. He regularly writes about topics related to coding, tech, politics, and sports. He is a regular columnist for various publications and magazines.

Sufyan is the CEO of Parakozm, a software development company catering to a global clientele. He is also the CTO at Samurai Servers, a web server management company focusing mainly on enterprise-scale audiences.

In his spare time, Sufyan teaches coding and English to young students.

> *There are many people that I wish to thank:*
> *Faisal Fareed and Sadaf Fareed, my siblings, for helping with things back home. The team at Packt, especially Hardik Bhinde, and others, for giving me the opportunity to review this book. The authors, and the Vue.js community, for all their hardwork and effort.*

Andrea Koutifaris has a passion for programming which he likes to say is in his DNA. At the age of thirteen, he began using his father's laptop to write his own programs. After graduating high school he enrolled, without a second thought, at the University of Florence, Faculty of Computer Engineering. After being a Java developer for some years, Andrea gradually moved to front-end development which is his passion till date. Having spent too much time fixing problems in messed up code, he is obsessed with good programming and test-driven development which, in his opinion, is the only way to write production quality code. Andrea has authored the book, Vuex Quick Start Guide, published recently by Packt.

Packt is searching for authors like you

If you're interested in becoming an author for Packt, please visit `authors.packtpub.com` and apply today. We have worked with thousands of developers and tech professionals, just like you, to help them share their insight with the global tech community. You can make a general application, apply for a specific hot topic that we are recruiting an author for, or submit your own idea.

Table of Contents

Preface

Up until a few years ago, direct DOM manipulation was the standard in frontend development, with jQuery leading the way. All that started changing with the popularization of modern JavaScript libraries and frameworks, mainly Angular and React. And then, in February of 2014, Vue came out with its initial release.

With large IT companies backing both Angular and React, it was not clear how Vue would carve out its position. Initially developed by a single developer, Evan You, in four short years—and without corporate backing—Vue went from being the fun little project of a single developer to an unlikely rival to the big boys, with over 300 contributors. It's not a one-man show anymore.

Today, Vue is used by NASA, GitLab, Alibaba, Grammarly, WizzAir, EuroNews, Xiaomi, Adobe, Behance, Nintendo, Chess.com, and many others.

Conclusion? Vue is here to stay. And while there might be an on-going discussion about whether it's better to learn Elm, or React, or Angular, or Ember, or something entirely different, this discussion is largely irrelevant. Each library and framework has something to offer, and in the end, it's simply a matter of trying it out and seeing whether it works for you.

We developers need to embrace the necessity to surf the technology wave and accept that learning new frameworks and paradigms is simply a part of our careers. Therefore, the question is not whether we should learn Vue, or any other battle-tested and proven tech out there.

Vue has already achieved its ranking, and it's playing in the same league with the big boys. The only question is, *How do I learn it efficiently?* and this book is an attempt to answer that question.

Who this book is for

This book is aimed at beginner-to-intermediate frontend web developers with no prior experience with Vue or other VDOM JavaScript libraries. It would be beneficial for readers to have some JavaScript and CSS knowledge. It is aimed at quickly bringing the reader up to speed regarding just how exactly Vue is set up and how its moving parts work together. It is meant to give you an overview of almost the entire Vue landscape, succinctly, and with lots of examples.

The goal of this book is simple – to quickly and efficiently introduce you to Vue and to ease you into the framework without a major investment of time and energy. The intended result is for you to have a huge return on investment – to gain enough practical knowledge of the framework that by the time you've read the book, which should not take long, you are confident to tackle some more advanced Vue projects and concepts.

What this book covers

Chapter 1, *Introducing Vue*, discusses what Vue is and gets started with mustache templates. We look at problems that Vue solves and reasons to use Vue.

Chapter 2, *Basic Concepts of Vue 2*, discusses reactivity, computed properties, and methods. We also introduce components, templates, props, watchers, and life cycle hooks.

Chapter 3, *Working with Vue-CLI, Components, Props, and Slots*, shows how to install vue-cli and how to set up code editors to work with Vue more effectively. We inspect the structure of a vue-cli-based project, look at how to add basic functionality to a child component, and look at passing data from children to parent components.

Chapter 4, *Filters and Mixins*, describes how to use filters. We look at syntax, use cases, and some examples. We also examine working with mixins.

Chapter 5, *Making Your Own Directives and Plugins*, looks at ways to extend Vue by making our own, custom directives. We also build our own plugin from scratch and learn how to publish it via npm.

Chapter 6, *Transitions and Animations*, takes the reader step by step from comparing CSS transitions with CSS animation to understanding the differences between them and how to start integrating them with Vue. We then discuss a myriad of ways to organize transitions and animations in Vue—with transition and transition-group components, with transition hooks as CSS classes, with named transition hooks, and with JavaScript transition hooks.

Chapter 7, *Using Vuex*, shows the reader, from the ground up, just exactly what state is and why it's important. It also explains the reasons to have the store – the centralized state – and how its internals work. We also tinker with some code examples of controlling our apps from this centralized store.

Chapter 8, *Using Nuxt.js and Vue-Router*, describes how SPAs work, what issues they have, and how these issues can be overcome with server-side rendering and code splitting. We then see how to build a very simple Nuxt.js app with a few pages, and some added transitions.

To get the most out of this book

This book will work for you best if you can do the following:

- Code basic HTML, CSS, and JavaScript
- Understand in general how the internet and browsers work
- Have some experience working with code editors and console programs
- Are willing to download examples (or fork them from CodePen)

The JavaScript code in this book is mostly written in ES5, but as the book progresses, sometimes ES6 has sneaked in. The reason for using ES5 is because it is not assumed that the reader understands ES6 syntax. Likewise, it is not assumed that readers have not used it before—hence, a compromise was made: not to focus on the features of ES6, but not to completely disregard them either. It is the author's humble opinion that this approach will shift the focus to where it matters: understanding Vue.

Download the example code files

You can download the example code files for this book from your account at `www.packt.com`. If you purchased this book elsewhere, you can visit `www.packt.com/support` and register to have the files emailed directly to you.

You can download the code files by following these steps:

1. Log in or register at `www.packt.com`.
2. Select the **SUPPORT** tab.
3. Click on **Code Downloads & Errata**.
4. Enter the name of the book in the **Search** box and follow the onscreen instructions.

Once the file is downloaded, please make sure that you unzip or extract the folder using the latest version of:

- WinRAR/7-Zip for Windows
- Zipeg/iZip/UnRarX for Mac
- 7-Zip/PeaZip for Linux

The code bundle for the book is also hosted on GitHub at `https://github.com/PacktPublishing/Vue.js-Quick-Start-Guide`. In case there's an update to the code, it will be updated on the existing GitHub repository.

We also have other code bundles from our rich catalog of books and videos available at `https://github.com/PacktPublishing/`. Check them out!

Download the color images

We also provide a PDF file that has color images of the screenshots/diagrams used in this book. You can download it here: `https://www.packtpub.com/sites/default/files/downloads/9781789344103_Color Images.pdf`.

Conventions used

There are a number of text conventions used throughout this book.

`CodeInText`: Indicates code words in text, database table names, folder names, filenames, file extensions, pathnames, dummy URLs, user input, and Twitter handles. Here is an example: "Mount the downloaded `WebStorm-10*.dmg` disk image file as another disk in your system."

A block of code is set as follows:

```
...
data: {
  // the model goes here
}
...
```

When we wish to draw your attention to a particular part of a code block, the relevant lines or items are set in bold:

```
div, .thetemplate {
  font-size: 30px;
  padding: 20px;
  color: limegreen;
  font-family: Arial;
```

Any command-line input or output is written as follows:

```
cd quickstart-vue
```

Bold: Indicates a new term, an important word, or words that you see onscreen. For example, words in menus or dialog boxes appear in the text like this. Here is an example: "Select **System info** from the **Administration** panel."

Warnings or important notes appear like this.

Tips and tricks appear like this.

Get in touch

Feedback from our readers is always welcome.

General feedback: If you have questions about any aspect of this book, mention the book title in the subject of your message and email us at customercare@packtpub.com.

Errata: Although we have taken every care to ensure the accuracy of our content, mistakes do happen. If you have found a mistake in this book, we would be grateful if you would report this to us. Please visit www.packt.com/submit-errata, selecting your book, clicking on the Errata Submission Form link, and entering the details.

Piracy: If you come across any illegal copies of our works in any form on the Internet, we would be grateful if you would provide us with the location address or website name. Please contact us at copyright@packt.com with a link to the material.

If you are interested in becoming an author: If there is a topic that you have expertise in and you are interested in either writing or contributing to a book, please visit authors.packtpub.com.

Reviews

Please leave a review. Once you have read and used this book, why not leave a review on the site that you purchased it from? Potential readers can then see and use your unbiased opinion to make purchase decisions, we at Packt can understand what you think about our products, and our authors can see your feedback on their book. Thank you!

For more information about Packt, please visit packt.com.

Introducing Vue

1

In this chapter, we will look into how to start learning Vue 2. This chapter will show you the easiest way to get started quickly and how to keep track of your progress easily with the help of the available SaaS platforms.

We will also look at why Vue is getting so popular, and why we should use it.

Furthermore, we'll discuss the basic building blocks of Vue: mustache templates, directives, modifiers, methods, and computed properties.

Along the way, we will look at a number of practical examples. Let's begin by looking at just what exactly Vue is.

In this chapter, we will take a look at the following topics:

- What is Vue?
- What problems does Vue solve?
- Why use Vue?

What is Vue?

Vue is a simple and easy-to-use JS framework which appeared in 2013. It is the successful result of taking some excellent ideas from Angular and React and combining them in an easy-to-use package.

Compared with other popular frontend frameworks, Vue comes out on top for simplicity and ease of use.

Let's see how we can start using it.

The quickest way to start using Vue2

In the last decade, a lot of the tools for web development have moved to the web, so let's go with the flow and start a new pen on `http://codepen.io/`.

You don't have to be a member of `https://codepen.io/` to create pens there—you can just save them with the blanket username `Captain Anonymous`. However, it's better to open an account so you have all your experiments in one place.

Once you navigate your browser to `https://codepen.io`, you'll be greeted with the following screen:

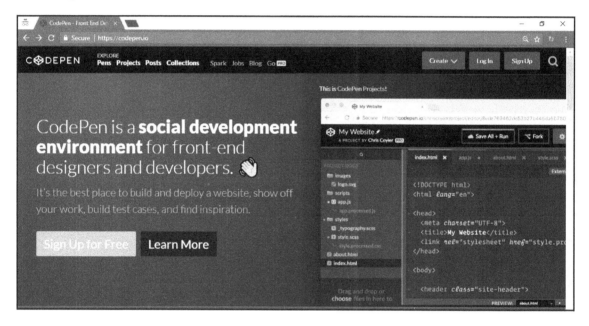

Click on the **Create** dropdown (in the main navigation, in the top-right area of the screen), and then click **New Pen**. Once you do, you will see the default editor setup:

Next, click the **Settings** button in the top right of the screen, and in the popup that appears choose **JavaScript**:

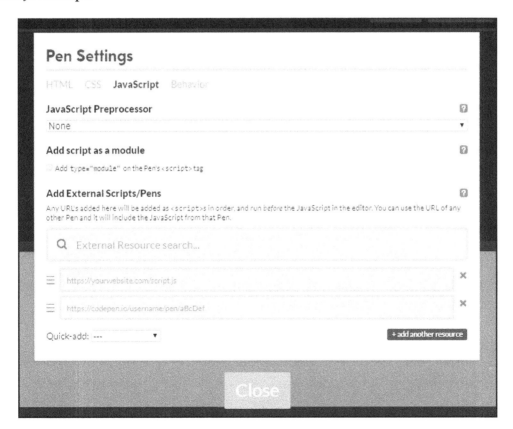

Next, in the **Quick-add** drop-down field, select the Vue option. Once you do, the first input will be filled out with the current minified version of Vue which is served from the Cloudflare CDN, or, more specifically, from this link: `https://cdnjs.cloudflare.com/ajax/libs/vue/2.5.13/vue.min.js`.

That's it! We're ready to start using Vue2 in our Codepen project.

One thing to understand about Vue is that it makes our HTML dynamic. This is achieved by adding **mustache syntax**. This syntax is very easy to understand. We simply insert it inside an HTML element. For example, we can add mustache syntax to an `h1` tag like this:

```
<h1>{{ heading1 }}</h1>
```

So, let's go over how this works in detail. Feel free to work on your own pen or see the example here: `https://codepen.io/AjdinImsirovic/pen/rKYyvE`.

Mustache template example

Let's begin working with our first pen:

```
<div id="entryPoint">
  <h1>Just an h1 heading here</h1>
  <h2>Just an h2 heading here</h2>
  <p>Vue JS is fun</p>
</div>
```

We can now see our HTML being rendered in the CodePen preview pane, with the following text printed on the screen:

Just an h1 heading here
Just an h2 heading here
Vue JS is fun

Note that the CodePen app will often update the preview pane even without saving, which is a lot better than refreshing the browser—that must be done when working on your projects locally. Still, it is good to save your CodePen projects often, to not lose any changes (in the odd case of your browser freezing or something else out of the ordinary happening).

Next, let's add the following Vue code to the JS pane inside our pen:

```
new Vue({
  el: '#entryPoint',
  data: {
```

```
      heading1: 'Just an h1 heading here',
      heading2: 'heading 2 here',
      paragraph1: 'Vue JS'
    }
})
```

Finally, let's update the HTML so that the Vue code can work its magic:

```
<div id="entryPoint">
  <h1>{{ heading1 }}</h1>
  <h2>Just an {{ heading2 }}</h2>
  <p>{{paragraph1}} is fun</p>
</div>
```

In the previous code example, we can see how we use mustache templates to dynamically insert data into our HTML.

 Mustache templating is achieved by simply passing the keys of our data object into our HTML tags and surrounding the keys with the opening {{ and closing }} tags.

As mentioned before, CodePen will auto-update the preview pane, but this will not affect the preview since we are effectively producing the same output as we did when we were using just plain HTML.

Now we can play with it simply by changing the key-value pairs inside our data entry:

```
new Vue({
  el: '#entryPoint',
  data: {
      heading1: 'This is an h1',
      heading2: 'h2 heading',
      paragraph1: 'Vue2'
  }
})
```

This time, the output will auto-update to this:

This is an h1
Just an h2 heading
Vue2 is fun

We can also change our entry point. For example, we can have Vue access only the `p` tag:

```
new Vue({
  el: 'p',
  data: {
     heading1: 'This is an h1',
     //heading2: 'h2 heading',
     paragraph1: 'Vue2'
  }
})
```

After this change, our preview pane will show the following:

{{ heading1 }}
Just an {{ heading2 }}
Vue2 is fun

From this output, we can conclude that our mustache templates will be rendered in our HTML output as regular text if either of the following things happen:

- Our entry point does not reference the data
- The entry in our data does not exist

We've also seen how our entry point can be any kind of selector. You can think of it as being similar to how you can target different elements in jQuery.

For example, we could have a more complex selector as our app's entry point:

```
new Vue({
  el: 'div#entryPoint',
  data: {
     heading1: 'This is an h1',
     heading2: 'h2 heading',
     paragraph1: 'Vue2'
  }
})
```

Using Vue's data option as a function

Note that the `data` option of our Vue instance can be either an object or a function. An example of data as an object can be seen in the previous code. Using data as a function is easy as well.

Data as an object doesn't work well with reusable components. For this reason, using data as a function is, generally speaking, a more useful way to use the data option in Vue.

Let's see another pen. This time, we'll use the data option as a function, instead of as an object. The pen is available here: `https://codepen.io/AjdinImsirovic/pen/aKVJgd`. The only change we'll make is in our Vue code:

```
new Vue({
  el: '#entryPoint',
  data() {
    return {
      heading1: 'Just an h1 heading here',
      heading2: 'heading 2 here',
      paragraph1: 'Vue JS data as a function'
    }
  }
})
```

Now that we're familiar with the very basics of Vue syntax, let's look at what it can be used for.

What problems does Vue solve?

Without trying to make an extensive list, let's quickly highlight some of Vue's greatest strengths:

- Vue—a jQuery successor?
- Vue is a great learning tool for beginners
- Vue is a versatile and progressive framework
- Vue is an awesome tool for animations and interactions
- Vue's approach is similar to other modern frontend frameworks and libraries

Next, let's briefly go over each of these points.

Vue, a jQuery successor

The famous jQuery library appeared in 2006. When it came out, it did a few things beautifully:

- It made writing cross-browser JavaScript a lot easier, which was a big plus at the time since it dramatically decreased the need for developers to mess with various browsers' quirks and inconsistencies
- It had a simple syntax that made it easier to target and manipulate specific DOM nodes, which is beautifully phrased in their motto *write less, do more*
- It was an excellent entry point to learning JavaScript in general
- It had a great API that made working with Ajax simple and easy

However, a lot has changed since then—for the better.

Arguably, the biggest improvement that happened in JavaScript-land between 2006 and today is the virtual DOM.

 The virtual DOM was a paradigm shift: we no longer had to write procedural, spaghetti JS to instruct the browser on how to traverse and manipulate the DOM. Instead of telling the browser *how* to update the DOM, we can now simply tell it *what* to update. Or, to be more specific, we tell *a framework* what to update—a framework like View or React. The actual implementation of the virtual DOM is framework-specific and not really something to be concerned with at this point.

We can now work with the DOM indirectly, by using *declarative* code that deals with the virtual DOM implementation of the underlying framework. This abstraction is the one thing that more or less made jQuery redundant.

Of course, since so many apps are still powered by jQuery and since legacy code has a tendency to stick around, jQuery *will* be alive and well in the years to come.

However, the paradigm shift in the way we think about DOM manipulation makes Vue a strong contender to jQuery's throne as the most popular game in town.

Vue also has other advantages: it is an excellent starting point to learn present-day frontend development. The barrier to entry is really low.

A learning tool for beginners

If a jQuery developer was faced with the option of learning either of the modern frontend frameworks/libraries, React, Angular, Vue, Ember... which one would probably be the easiest to get started with?

Vue, of course!

As we've seen already, getting started with Vue can be as simple as importing a CDN. And since we humans are wired to thrive on small, frequent victories, Vue seems to be the happy route to take. This is not to say that a developer should not try to learn other frontend frameworks too. It just seems that Vue is the easiest way to get started and the best way to get productive quickly.

A versatile and progressive framework

The official website for Vue JS says that Vue is *the Progressive JavaScript Framework*. This means you can add Vue to an existing server-side project incrementally. Basically, you can add Vue to just one simple section of your website. No wonder Laravel chose to bundle with Vue on its frontend.

But you don't have to settle for only sprinkling Vue in here and there. You can also extend it using Vuex and Vue-Router. This makes Vue very versatile and usable in a number of different scenarios.

A tool for animations and transitions

If you need to make high-performance animations and transitions, look no further than Vue! Vue's animations API is very easy to understand and it's a joy to use. It is so easy to do animations in Vue that you will be amazed at how much you can accomplish in a very short time.

Features similar to other modern frontend frameworks and libraries

Just like other modern frontend frameworks, such as React and Angular, Vue has the following:

- Virtual DOM
- A command-line interface (Vue-cli)
- State management (Vuex)
- Routing (Vue-Router)

However, it seems that Vue's core team is going out of their way to make Vue as approachable as possible. This is evident in several examples:

- The effort they've put in to avoid the hassle of setting up Vue-cli, which makes it very easy to get started with
- The lack of complicated toolchains
- The simplicity of Vue's API

Like the official project's website states, Vue is approachable, versatile, and performant.

Why use Vue?

We have discussed the problems that Vue solves in the previous section. In this section, we will look at practical examples of why it is a pleasure to work with:

- Declarative code (we tell Vue what to do, not how to do it)
- Easy to understand syntax (it's as minimal as it can get)
- Feels like a right fit for a variety of projects

Declarative code

Let's compare vanilla JavaScript code with Vue JavaScript code.

For this example, we'll print out members of an array.

In vanilla JavaScript, this will be the code:

```html
<!DOCTYPE html>
<html lang="en">
<head>
  <meta charset="UTF-8">
  <title>Document</title>
  <style>
    .list-item {
      background: white;
      color: gray;
      padding: 20px;
      margin: 20px;
    }
  </style>
</head>
<body>
  <script>
    var arr1 = ['a','b','c'];
    var unorderedList = document.createElement('ul');
    unorderedList.style.cssText = "background:tomato; width:
    400px;height:400px";
    document.body.appendChild(unorderedList);
    for (var i=0; i<3; i++) {
      var listItem = document.createElement('li');
      listItem.className = "list-item";
      unorderedList.appendChild(listItem);
      listItem.innerHTML = arr1[i];
    }
  </script>
</body>
</html>
```

In this file, the focus should be on the code inside the `script` tags.

You can see this example in the form of a pen at this URL: `https://codepen.io/AjdinImsirovic/pen/xzPdxO`.

There are several things that we are doing in this code:

1. We are setting `array1`, which will later populate the list items we will create dynamically
2. We are creating a `ul`—an unordered list element that will wrap all our list items (all our `li` elements)
3. We are setting the styles for our `ul`

4. We are appending `unorderedList` to the body of our document
5. Next, we use a `for` loop to create three `li` elements
6. Still inside the `for` loop, we add a class to each list item
7. We then append each of them to the unordered list element
8. Finally, we add `innerHTML` to each list item

Many objections could be made to the way that this code is made. We could have used a `forEach`; we could have avoided adding styles the way we did and instead called the CSS from a separate file. But the biggest objection is how fragile this code is. Let's contrast this code with the same thing written in Vue.

In Vue, our code will look like this:

```
<!-- HTML -->
<ul>
  <li v-for="entry in entries">
    {{ entry.content }}
  </li>
</ul>

// JS
var listExample = new Vue ({
  el: "ul",
  data: {
    entries: [
      { content: 'a'},
      { content: 'b'},
      { content: 'c'}
    ]
  }
})
```

The code for this example can be found here: `https://codepen.io/AjdinImsirovic/pen/VdrbYW`.

As we can see at just a simple glance, Vue's code is a lot easier to understand and reason about in comparison to the same code implemented in vanilla JavaScript.

> The `el` here is the entry point for our Vue app. The `data` option is the actual data our Vue app will work with.

There's also another major benefit to this setup: once you understand how Vue works, any other project that uses Vue will simply make sense to you, which will yield increased productivity and efficiency.

The Vue way of doing things thus promotes being faster and doing more things in less time.

Feels like a right fit for a variety of projects

One of the strengths of Vue is the possibility of incremental implementation. If you would just like to make a quick, simple experiment in Vue, no problems. You can start with Vue in under a minute, literally.

This makes it great for converting legacy projects, building projects from scratch, or for simple experiments.

Vue is also maturing quickly. There is a vibrant Vue community and a lot of developers are working on it continuously. For example, one of the arguments for people to choose React over Vue was the lack of a framework to build native mobile apps in Vue. That's no longer the case: Vue Native is available as of June 2018. You can check it out at `https://github.com/GeekyAnts/vue-native-core`, or find out more about it at `https://vue-native.io/`.

With all of this in mind, there are plenty of reasons why learning Vue is a nice return on investment for anyone, especially frontend developers.

Easy-to-understand syntax

One thing that can be noticed in this example of a very simple Vue app is the use of the `v-for` HTML attribute.

Directives

All the `v-*` attributes in Vue are called *directives*, which is borrowed from Angular.

The concept of directives is very interesting. They make code easier to understand, easier to think about, and easier to work with.

There are other directives in Vue that we will use extensively throughout this book. For now, let's just list some of them: `v-bind`, `v-cloak`, `v-for`, `v-else`, `v-else-if`, `v-model`, `v-on`, `v-once`, `v-text`, and `v-html`.

An example of a useful directive is `v-model`. The `v-model` directive is used to make forms reactive; it helps us update data on user input events. While this topic might sound a bit advanced to a beginner in Vue, this complexity is dealt with so elegantly that even beginners should find it easy to see what is happening in the code:

```html
<!-- HTML -->
<div id="app">
  <span>Enter the weight in kilograms:</span>
  <input v-model="someNum" type="number">
  <div>The weight in pounds is: {{ someNum * 2.20 }}</div>
</div>

// js
new Vue({
  el: '#app',
  data() {
    return {
      someNum: "1"
    }
  }
})
```

As you can see, the `{{ someNum }}` value is bound to whatever a user types into the input field. In other words, the underlying data model—the value of `someNum`—will change based on user input.

To view the pen for the preceding example, visit `https://codepen.io/AjdinImsirovic/pen/pKdPgX`.

Modifiers

The directives in Vue are further extended with the help of modifiers.

The link to official documentation on modifiers in directives can be found at this link: `https://vuejs.org/v2/guide/forms.html#Modifiers`.

To use a modifier, we simply append it to a directive. The simplest possible example might look a bit like this:

```html
<!-- HTML -->
<div>
  <input v-model.trim="userInput" placeholder="type here">
  <p>You have typed in: {{ userInput }}</p>
</div>
```

```
// js
new Vue({
  el: 'div',
  data() {
    return {
      userInput: ""
    }
  }
})
```

We have just appended the `trim` modifier to the `v-model` directive.

You can view the example for this code at this link: `https://codepen.io/AjdinImsirovic/pen/eKeRXK`.

This modifier will trim any whitespace (such as spaces or tabs) typed into the input field by the user.

Before continuing with this 10,000-foot overview of Vue syntax, let's also mention the `v-on` directive, which is used for event handling. Here is a quick example:

```
<!-- HTML -->
<div id="example-1">
  <button v-on:click="counter += 1">Add 1</button>
  <p>The button above has been clicked {{ counter }} times.</p>
</div>

// JS
var example1 = new Vue({
  el: '#example-1',
  data: {
    counter: 0
  }
})
```

Vue even provides shortcut syntax for `v-on`: the `@` symbol. Thus, we can replace `v-on:click` with just `@click` and our Vue counter will still work.

To view this example in `http://codepen.io/`, visit the following URL: `https://codepen.io/AjdinImsirovic/pen/PaOjvz`.

Vue methods

The `methods` option in a Vue instance just lists all the functions that exist on that Vue instance (or on a Vue component).

The `methods` option works with the data of the Vue instance. What follows is a simple demonstration of this concept in practice:

```
// HTML
<div id="definitions">
  <!-- 'whatIsVue' and 'whyUseVue' are functions defined in the 'methods'
option in the Vue instance -->
  <button id="btn" v-on:click="whatIsVue">What is Vue?</button>
  <button id="btn" v-on:click="whyUseVue">Why use Vue?</button>
</div>

// JS
var definitions = new Vue({
 el: '#definitions',
 data: {
 name: 'Vue.js'
 },
 // define methods (functions) under the `methods` object
 methods: {
   whatIsVue: function () {
    console.info(this.name + ' is a Progressive Front-end Framework')
   },
   whyUseVue: function () {
    alert('Because ' + this.name + ' is nice.')
   }
 }
})
```

As we can see, the `data` option holds the `Vue.js` string, which can be accessed via the `name` key.

Inside the `methods` option, we can see two functions: `whatIsVue` and `whyUseVue`. The `whatIsVue` function takes the click event and logs out the value inside `name` to the console. The `whyUseVue` function inside the `methods` option works similarly.

This code can be seen in a pen at this address: `https://codepen.io/AjdinImsirovic/pen/yEPXdK`.

Computed properties and watchers

Computed properties are used to avoid complex logic adding bloat to your views. In other words, computed properties are useful to hide the complexity from our HTML and thus keep our HTML understandable, easy to use, and declarative. Put differently, when we need to compute some values from the `data` option, we can do that with the help of computed properties.

The full code for the following example can be seen at `https://codepen.io/AjdinImsirovic/pen/WyXEOz`:

```html
<!-- HTML -->
<div id="example">
  <p>User name: "{{ message }}"</p>
  <p>Message prefixed with a title: "{{ prefixedMessage }}"</p>
</div>
```

```js
// JS
var example = new Vue({
  el: '#example',
  data: {
    userName: 'John Doe',
    title: ''
  },
  computed: {
    // a computed getter
    prefixedMessage: function () {
      // `this` points to the Vue instance's data option
      return this.title + " " + this.userName
    }
  }
})
```

 Computed properties are cached. As long as a computed property's dependencies do not change, Vue will return the cached value of the computed property.

Watchers are not as frequently used as computed properties are. In other words, the watch option is to be used less frequently than the computed properties option. Watchers are commonly used for asynchronous or otherwise costly operations with changing data.

Watchers have to do with reactive programming; they allow us to observe a sequence of events through time and react to changes as they happen on a certain data property.

We will cover the subject of computed properties and watchers in later chapters. For now, it is sufficient to know that they exist in Vue and that they are widely used.

Summary

In this chapter, we looked at how to get started with Vue quickly, with the help of `codepen.io`. We also discussed some of the most important ideas and concepts in Vue, such as the quickest and most developer-friendly way to start learning Vue 2. We looked into what problems Vue solves, what its strengths are, and why it is sometimes referred to as *the new jQuery*. We learned about mustache templates, Vue's declarative code, and its easy-to-understand syntax. Finally, we introduced directives, modifiers, methods, computed properties, and watchers.

In the next chapter, we will see what reactive programming is and how it is applied in Vue. We will also look at further expanding the concepts covered in this chapter, and we will introduce some additional features of Vue.

Basic Concepts of Vue 2

In this chapter, we will discuss data-driven views in Vue. We will also examine how DOM is manipulated with the help of directives. Next, we'll learn what components are and how to create them, and we'll cover concepts related to templates, methods, data, computed properties, and watchers.

All components have a life cycle, and we have special methods to access a component at certain points of its life. These methods are called **lifecycle hooks**, and we'll examine them in this chapter too.

In this chapter, we will learn about the following:

- Data-driven views in Vue
- Computed properties and methods and how to use them
- Understanding components, templates, and props
- Ways of building component templates in Vue
- Quickly prototyping websites with the help of Vue components and v-* directives
- Utilizing watchers in Vue
- The importance of lifecycle hooks and how to plug into this functionality in Vue

Data-driven views in Vue

Data-driven views in Vue are achieved with the help of reactivity.

What is reactivity?

To grasp the concept better, let's look at an example code in which there is no reactivity. We will use an example that is very similar to the one we had in the previous chapter, when we were comparing Vue and vanilla JS. In the original example, using JavaScript, we created an unordered list and three list items inside of it. The values of the three list items were added from an array we declared, and the unordered list was populated with these list items using a for loop.

This time, we will do something slightly different. To see the example as a pen, visit https://codepen.io/AjdinImsirovic/pen/JZOZdR.

In this non-reactive example, we are predefining the members of the array as variables. Then we populate the array with those variables and print them to the screen as list items of an unordered list that gets appended to the document:

```
var a = 1;
var b = a + 1;
var c = b + 2;
var arr1 = [a,b,c];
var unorderedList = document.createElement('ul');
document.body.appendChild(unorderedList);
for (var i=0; i<3; i++) {
  var listItem = document.createElement('li');
  listItem.className = "list-item";
  unorderedList.appendChild(listItem);
  listItem.innerHTML = arr1[i];
}
arr1[0] = 2;
for (var i=0; i<3; i++) {
  var listItem = document.createElement('li');
  listItem.className = "list-item";
  unorderedList.appendChild(listItem);
  listItem.innerHTML = arr1[i];
}
```

However, what happens when we change a member of the array and repeat the for loop a second time? As we can see in the pen, the first and the fourth list items are different. The first value is 1, and the second value is 2. To make it more obvious, these items are in bold red text and have a gray background. The first value is the initial value of var a. The second value is the value of var a, updated with this line of code: arr1[0] = 2.

However, the values of variables b and c are not updated in the second for loop, even though we defined variables b and c in terms of variable a increased by 1 and 2, respectively.

So, we can see that there is no reactivity in JavaScript out of the box.

As far as Vue is concerned, reactivity is the term that is used to refer to the way in which Vue tracks changes. In other words, reactivity is the way in which changes in state are reflected in the DOM. Practically, this means that when a change is made to data, that change will be propagated to the page so that the user can see it. Therefore, saying that *Vue is reactive* is the same as saying *Vue tracks changes*. As a concept, it's as simple as that.

How does Vue achieve this?

Vue stores its data in the data option, which is either a function or an object:

```
...
data: {
  // the model goes here
}
...
```

Any change in the data model is reflected in the view (on the screen). Vue achieves this reactivity with the help of getters and setters. When the data object is received by the Vue instance, all the properties of the data object will be updated as getters and setters. This is done with the help of the Object.defineProperty API.

Computed properties and methods

The usefulness of reactivity in Vue can be described in terms of the difference between computed properties and methods.

As we mentioned earlier, a Vue instance can have either computed properties, methods, or both computed properties and methods. So, what is the difference between the two?

Methods are simply run every time they are called. On the other hand, computed properties are cached, meaning they are only run when the underlying data model changes. This is often described in terms of computed property dependencies. Also, methods can have parameters, whereas computed properties cannot.

What exactly are these dependencies?

Consider this simple Vue app, available as a pen at this link: `https://codepen.io/AjdinImsirovic/pen/qKVyry`.

This is the code of the simple app:

```
<!--HTML-->
<div id="example">
  <p>Enter owner name and the thing that is owned:
    <input v-model="ownerName" placeholder="enter owner">
    <input v-model="thing" placeholder="enter thing">
  </p>
  <span>{{ ownerName }}</span>
  <span> has a </span>
  <span>{{ thing }}</span>
</div>

// JS
var example = new Vue({
  el: '#example',
  data: {
    ownerName: 'e.g Old McDonald',
    thing: 'e.g cow'
  },
  computed: {
    // a computed getter
    ownerHasThing: function () {
      // `this` points to the Vue instance's data option
      return this.ownerName + " " + this.thing
    }
  }
})
```

This code will result in this output on the screen:

Enter owner name and the thing that is owned: enter owner	enter thing
has a	

First off, we can see that there is this weird **has a** line of text in the view. This problem here is that we have not used our `ownerHasThing` computed property. In other words, these three lines in HTML are completely redundant:

```
<span>{{ ownerName }}</span>
<span> has a </span>
<span>{{ thing }}</span>
```

Also, what if we wanted to run a computed property only after both the input fields have been filled out and the focus has been moved out of the inputs or the *Enter* key was pressed?

This might seem like a relatively complex thing to achieve. Luckily, in Vue it is very easy.

Let's look at the updated code (also available as a pen here: `https://codepen.io/ AjdinImsirovic/pen/aKVjqj`):

```
<!--HTML-->
<div id="example">
  <p>Enter owner name:
    <input v-model.lazy="ownerName" placeholder="enter owner">
  </p>
  <p>Enter thing owned:
    <input v-model.lazy="thing" placeholder="enter thing">
  </p>
  <h1 v-if="ownerName && thing">{{ ownerHasThing }}</h1>
</div>
```

The JavaScript code is only slightly different:

```
var example = new Vue({
  el: '#example',
  data: {
    ownerName: '',
    thing: ''
  },
  computed: {
    // a computed getter
    ownerHasThing: function () {
      // `this` points to the Vue instance's data option
      return this.ownerName + " has a " + this.thing
    }
  }
})
```

We can conclude from this that computed properties are simply data dependencies that have some computations performed on them. In other words, `ownerHasThing` is a computed property, and its dependencies are `ownerName` and `thing`.

Whenever `ownerName` or `thing` are changed, the `ownerHasThing` computed property will update as well.

However, the `ownerHasThing` will not update always, since it is cached. Contrary to this, a method will always update; that is, it will always be run, regardless of whether the data model has changed or not.

This might not seem like a very important difference, but consider a situation in which your method needs to fetch data from a third-party API or it has a lot of code to run. This might slow things down, and that's why in such cases, using computed properties is the way to go.

Before we conclude this section, let's quickly go over the code in the previous example.

In HTML, we are using `v-model.lazy`. The `lazy` modifier waits for the user to either click outside of the input or press the *Enter* key on their keyboard, or otherwise leave the input field (such as by pressing the *Tab* key).

Still in HTML, we are also using the `v-if` directive, and we give it `ownerName && thing`. Then, we add mustache templates: `{{ ownerHasThing }}`. The `v-if` directive will wait until both `ownerName` and `thing` are updated in the data object. So, once that both inputs are filled out and no longer in focus, does the computed property update the underlying data model, and only then is the `{{ ownerHasThing }}` message printed on the screen.

In the next section, we'll look at how we can work with templates and components.

Understanding components, templates, and props

To begin, let's look at how to make a component in Vue. First, we specify the component, like this:

```
Vue.component('custom-article', {
  template: `
    <article>
      Our own custom article component!<span></span>
    </article>`
})
```

```
new Vue({
    el: '#app'
})
```

A component is a block of code that we give a custom name. This custom name can be anything we come up with, and it's *a single label for that entire block of code* in the form of a custom HTML tag. In the previous example, we grouped the `article` and `span` tags and gave that custom tag the name of `custom-article`.

> Components are named using kebab-case.

The code for this component is available as a Codepen at `https://codepen.io/AjdinImsirovic/pen/xzpOaJ`.

Now, to create an instance of our component, we simply use our `<custom-article>` opening and closing tags in our HTML, like this:

```
<main id="app">
    <custom-article></custom-article>
</main>
```

> Our custom-article component is referred to as the *child* component.
>
> The parent is the actual Vue instance.

Note that you can use string templates even without a component. You simply add the template option to your Vue instance, like this:

```
//HTML
<main id="app"></main>
//JS
new Vue({
  el: '#app',
  template: '<article>A string template without a
component!<span></span></article>'
})
```

The example code for the previous example is available here: `https://codepen.io/AjdinImsirovic/pen/RJxMae`.

Next, we'll see how we can improve our component with the help of the `props` and `data` options.

Adding props and data for better components

To make our `custom-article` component more useful, we'll add a `props` option to it, like this:

```
Vue.component('custom-article', {
  props: ['content'],
  template: '<article>{{content}}</article>'
})
new Vue({
  el: '#app'
})
```

Props are a way to pass the data from the parent to the child. They are one-way flows of data between the parent and the child. Props are always defined as an array.

The code for the previous example is available here: `https://codepen.io/AjdinImsirovic/pen/KeZNPr`.

We have registered a prop in our component, and now we can use it in HTML as an attribute named just like our prop:

```
<main id="app">
  <custom-article content="This component was made with the help of a prop.">
  </custom-article>
</main>
```

Props are used when we need to make smaller changes to our components without having to make a whole new component. They help us reuse what we already have.

In the next section, we'll use the Vue instance's `data` object to add content to our `custom-article` component.

Adding content to our components with the help of the data object

The code pen for this example can be found at `https://codepen.io/AjdinImsirovic/pen/QxadmE`.

In our HTML, we'll change the code to the following:

```
<main id="app">
  <custom-article v-bind:content="datacontent">
  </custom-article>
</main>
```

In our JS, we'll update our Vue code to this:

```
Vue.component('custom-article', {
  props: ['content'],
  template: '<article>{{content}}</article>'
})
new Vue({
    el: '#app',
    data: {
      datacontent: 'This component was made with the help of a data object
in the Vue instance'
    }
})
```

In the previous example, we are using the v-bind directive to bind the content prop in our custom-article component to the datacontent property of our data object.

 If you think through this code, you will see that props are almost like named variables (with the prop's variable name being content in the example). Props simply pass to the child component whatever data they receive from the parent.

There is also another way we can do this. Instead of using data inside our Vue instance, we can give it to our component; only this time it has to be a data function. Here is the full code for this implementation:

```
// HTML
<main id="app">
  <custom-article></custom-article>
</main>

// JS
Vue.component('custom-article', {
  template: '<article>{{datacontent}}</article>',
  data: function() {
    return {
      datacontent: 'This component was made with the help of a data
function in the Vue component called custom-article'
    }
  }
```

```
})
new Vue({
    el: '#app'
})
```

To view the pen for the previous example, visit `https://codepen.io/AjdinImsirovic/pen/VdyQzW`.

 If we used data as an object instead of as a function, then reactivity would apply to all instances of our component. Since the main purpose of components is to be reusable, it is important to remember that in this case data must be a function.

Props can also be defined as objects, which allows us to give them a lot more information: validate incoming data, set default values in case no data comes through, and so on.

In the following example, we are stating that our `custom-article` component is expecting the parent to pass it a prop named `message`, or type string, which is required:

```
<!--HTML-->
<div id="app">
  <custom-article :message-being-passed="datacontent"></custom-article>
</div>

//JS
Vue.component('custom-article', {
  props: {
    messageBeingPassed: {
      type: String,
      required: true,
      default: 'Hello Vue'
    }
  },
  template: `<div class="thetemplate">{{ message }}</div>`
});

new Vue({
  el: "#app",
  data: function() {
    return {
      datacontent: 'This component was made with the help of a data
function in the Vue component called custom-article, and the data passed
was validated with the help of the props object inside the Vue component'
    }
  }
})
```

```
//CSS
.thetemplate {
  font-size: 30px;
  padding: 20px;
  color: limegreen;
  font-family: Arial;
  border: 3px solid green;
  border-radius: 10px;
}
```

This example is available at `https://codepen.io/AjdinImsirovic/pen/mKpxGZ`.

Let's say we commented out the `datacontent` property of the Vue instance's `data` function. Can you guess what would happen?

In other words, what would happen if `datacontent` is not providing the correct data? The child component will simply revert to its `default` property in the `props` object.

To see this in action, visit this link: `https://codepen.io/AjdinImsirovic/pen/BVJxKL`.

Other ways of building component templates in Vue

So far, we have looked at defining templates as strings (using single or double quotes) and as template literals (using backticks). There are also many other ways to work with component templates:

- Inline templates
- X-templates
- Render functions
- Single file components
- JSX

Most of them have their pros and cons. For example, using JSX in Vue is possible but generally frowned upon, as it in not the Vue way of doing things. Inline templates are made using the `inline-template` attribute in your HTML.

If you add `type=''text/x-template''` to an HTML script tag, you will make a Vue x-template. Here's an example:

```
// HTML
<div id="app">
  <script type="text/x-template" id="custom-article-template">
    <p>{{ name }}</p>
  </script>
</div>

// JS
Vue.component('custom-article', {
  template: '#custom-article-template',
  props: ['name']
})
new Vue({
    el: '#app'
})
```

The code pen for this example is available here: `https://codepen.io/AjdinImsirovic/pen/NzXyem`.

Single-file templates are probably the most practical way of creating templates in Vue. You keep all your HTML, JS, and styling in a single file (with a `.vue` file extension), and you compile this file with a build process, such as Webpack. We will look into this in later chapters when we cover the use of Webpack in Vue (with the help of Vue-cli).

Building a simple web page out of components

As we have seen in the previous section, there are many ways to build a component in Vue, which might make things look more complex than they have to be. While it is important to be aware of the versatility that Vue brings to the various ways we can build components, in this section we will look at a simple way to use components to build a web page.

Before we begin building out our page, one thing should be clear to us: each component in Vue is also just another Vue instance. This means that each component takes an options object, which has the same key value pairs as any other Vue instance. The only difference to this rule is that the root Vue instance has some additional options that can only be used in it.

After these introductory clarifications, let's see how a component can be added to a Vue instance.

Adding simple components to a Vue instance

To start off this example, we'll begin with a simple Vue instance.

In our JavaScript file, let's make the simplest possible Vue instance, with the `#app` element as its entry point:

```
new Vue({
  el: '#app',
  data: {}
})
```

Next, let's add just one div in our HTML, so that our Vue instance has an element in our page to get access to its DOM:

```
<div id="app"></div>
```

Now we will add another component to our JavaScript file. Let's extend our existing JS file by adding the following code to the very top:

```
Vue.component('the-header', {
  template: '<h1 class="header css classes go here">Our example
header</h1>'
})
```

Now we can simply add the custom `the-header` component inside our HTML:

```
<div id="app">
  <the-header></the-header>
</div>
```

Doing this will render **Our example header** text on the screen.

Now that we have seen just how easy it is to add one simple component to our Vue apps, let's add another one to drive the point home.

We'll start by extending our JS file with another component, `the-footer`:

```
Vue.component('the-header', {
  template: '<h1 class="header css classes go here">Our example
header</h1>'
});

Vue.component('the-footer', {
  template: '<h1 class="footer css classes go here">Our example
header</h1>'
});
```

```
//Root Instance
new Vue({
  el: '#app',
  data: {}
})
```

Of course, we need to update our HTML in order to make this work:

```
<div id="app">
  <the-header></the-header>
  <the-footer></the-footer>
</div>
```

When naming custom components, we need to use hyphens. This is done to make sure there are no naming collisions with regular HTML elements.

The example code for this section is available at `https://codepen.io/AjdinImsirovic/pen/qypBbz`.

Now that we understand how to add a simple component to our Vue instance, let's practice by adding a more complex example.

Creating a more complex page out of components in Vue

To begin, let's add a single component to our new Vue instance. This time, we will employ the data option inside our custom component's options object.

This is the code we start with:

```
Vue.component('the-header', {
  template: '<h1 class="h1 text-success">{{header}}</h1>',
  data: function() {
    return {
      header: 'Just another simple header'
    }
  }
});

//Root Instance
new Vue({
  el: '#app',
  data: {}
})
```

In this code, we have added mustache syntax to our template. Then we have utilized the data option to return the text, which will be interpolated in the template. The mustache syntax tells our component to look for the `header` inside our data option.

The code for this example is available here: `https://codepen.io/AjdinImsirovic/pen/wxpvxy`.

Next, under our header, we'll add some Bootstrap cards.

For simplicity's sake, we'll use an existing example from the official Bootstrap documentation, which is available at the following URL: `https://getbootstrap.com/docs/4.0/components/card/#using-grid-markup`.

The example provides the following code:

```
<div class="row">
  <div class="col-sm-6">
    <div class="card">
      <div class="card-body">
        <h5 class="card-title">Special title treatment</h5>
        <p class="card-text">
          With supporting text below as a natural lead-in to additional
          content.
        </p>
        <a href="#" class="btn btn-primary">Go somewhere</a>
      </div>
    </div>
  </div>
  <div class="col-sm-6">
    <div class="card">
      <div class="card-body">
        <h5 class="card-title">Special title treatment</h5>
        <p class="card-text">
          With supporting text below as a natural lead-in to additional
          content.
        </p>
        <a href="#" class="btn btn-primary">Go somewhere</a>
      </div>
    </div>
  </div>
</div>
```

Although the Bootstrap framework is not the subject of this book, it will be useful for us to give a real-world example of using Vue components in practice. Since Bootstrap has basically become the industry standard for frontend frameworks, it is the perfect candidate for showing not only how Vue components are used in general, but also how they can be incorporated with other frontend technologies.

Now let's see how we can add a single card to our example Vue webpage. This is the code to add to our JS:

```
Vue.component('the-card', {
  template: '<div class="card"><div class="card-body"><h5 class="card-title">Special title treatment</h5><p class="card-text">With supporting text below as a natural lead-in to additional content.</p><a href="#" class="btn btn-primary">Go somewhere</a></div></div></div>',
});
```

The code for this stage of the development of our code is available here: `https://codepen.io/AjdinImsirovic/pen/VByYeW`.

Next, let's add our card component to our HTML. The full updated code will look like this:

```
<div id="app">
 <div class="container">
    <the-header></the-header>
    <div class="row">
      <div class="col-sm-6">
        <the-card></the-card>
      </div>
      <div class="col-sm-6">
        <the-card></the-card>
      </div>
    </div>
  </div>
</div>
```

Adding the previous code to our HTML, with the JS updates already in place as described earlier, we will get the following result:

We have added a single card component in our JS; however, as we can see in the previous example, we can now reuse it in our HTML as many times as needed.

This gives us an excellent opportunity to quickly prototype complete web pages with the help of Vue.

We can take it even one step further, as we'll see in the next section.

Improving our Vue-based layouts with v-for

In this section, we will improve our existing web page with the help of Vue directives.

Our specific goal is to try to use the data option in our component instance and combine it with the powers of Vue directives to further improve our Vue apps.

The code for this section is available at `https://codepen.io/AjdinImsirovic/pen/Epoamy`.

Let's make our JS a bit easier to read with the help of the backtick ES6 JS syntax. This syntax allows us to write JavaScript strings which span multiple lines:

```js
Vue.component('the-header', {
  template: '<h1 class="h1 text-success">{{header}}</h1>',
  data: function() {
    return {
      header: 'Just another simple header'
    }
  }
});

Vue.component('the-card', {
  template: `
    <div class="card">
      <div class="card-body">
        <h5 class="card-title">Special title treatment</h5>
        <p class="card-text">
          With supporting text below as a natural lead-in to addtional
          content.
        </p>
        <a href="#" class="btn btn-primary">Go somewhere</a>
      </div>
    </div>`,
});

//Root Instance
new Vue({
  el: '#app',
```

```
      data: {}
})
```

Now, let's add the `data` option to the `the-card` Vue component:

```
data: function() {
  return {
    customCard: [{
      heading: 'John Doe',
      text: 'John.doe@acme.org'
    },
    {
      heading: 'John Doe',
      text: 'John.doe@acme.org'
    }
  ]}
}
```

As we can see in the preceding code, we are returning a `customCard` array of objects, with each object holding a specific `heading` and `text`.

Next, we can use the `v-for` directive in our template, like this:

```
Vue.component('the-card', {
  template: `
    <div class="card">
      <div class="card-body" v-for="customCard in customCards">
        <h5 class="card-title">{{customCard.heading}}</h5>
        <p class="card-text">
          {{customCard.text}}
        </p>
        <a href="#" class="btn btn-primary">Go somewhere</a>
      </div>
    </div>`,
```

We introduce the `v-for` directive in the `div` that has the class of `card-body`. We loop through each `customCard` in our collection of `customCards`, and we interpolate the `h5` text's content with `customCard.heading` for each object of our `customCard` array.

Finally, let's add a Bootstrap class to our HTML so that the `h1` tag of our web page is not glued to the very top of the viewport. For that, we will use Bootstrap's spacing utilities. You can read about them here: `https://getbootstrap.com/docs/4.0/utilities/spacing/`.

The change in our HTML will be minimal, with just an addition of another CSS class: `mt-5`.

Finally, what follows is the complete JS code for the improved page. First, we register the main title component:

```
//Register main title component
Vue.component("main-title-component", {
  template: '<h1 class="text-center mt-5 mb-4">{{title}}</h1>',
  data: function() {
    return {
      title: "Just another title"
    };
  }
});
```

Then we register the `list group` component:

```
//Register list group component
Vue.component("list-group-component", {
  template: `
    <ul class="list-group">
      <li class="list-group-item" v-for="item in
items">{{item.description}}</li>
    </ul>`,
  data: function() {
    return {
      items: [
        {
          description: "Description one"
        },
        {
          description: "Description two"
        },
        {
          description: "Description three"
        }
      ]
    };
  }
});
```

After that, we register the `card` component:

```
// Register card component
Vue.component("card-component", {
  template: `
    <div class="card">
      <div class="card-body">
        <h5 class="card-title">{{title}}</h5>
        <p class="card-text">{{text}}</p>
```

```
            <a href="#" class="btn btn-primary">Go somewhere</a>
        </div>
    </div>`,
    data: function() {
      return {
        title: "This is the card title",
        text: "This is the card text"
      };
    }
});
```

We also add the `root instance`:

```
//root Instance
new Vue({
  el: "#app",
    data: {}
});
```

And here is the HTML:

```
<div id="app">
  <div class="container mt-5 mb-5">
    <main-title-component></main-title-component>
    <div class="row">
      <div class="col">
        <list-group-component></list-group-component>
      </div>
      <div class="col">
        <card-component></card-component>
      </div>
    </div>
  </div>
</div>
```

The result of adding the previous code can be seen in this screenshot:

In this section, we have looked at components and how to get started with using them. Next, we'll discuss watchers in Vue.

Watchers in Vue

Every component in Vue has a watcher.

To understand how this works, let's begin with an earlier example from this chapter. The example is from the *Computed properties* section, at this link: `https://codepen.io/AjdinImsirovic/pen/qKVyry`. That is our starting code. As we know from the previous section, we have two input fields here and we are printing out the values entered into these input fields in some span tags under the form.

Let's extend our example. The initial code is the same; we will only be adding a watcher to it. The updated code can be found at this Codepen URL: `https://codepen.io/AjdinImsirovic/pen/jprwKe`.

As can be observed, the only update we made to the original pen is the addition of the watchers option, as follows:

```
watch: {
  ownerName(previousValue,currentValue) {
    console.log(`The value in the first input has changed from:
      ${previousValue} to: ${currentValue}`);
  }
},
```

How does the previous watcher work? It allows us to use a method that must have the same name as the computed property we are watching in our HTML. The watcher has optional parameters we can pass to it to be worked with in the body of the method; in this case, we gave our optional parameters some nice and descriptive names: `previousValue` and `currentValue`.

In the body of the `watch` method, we are logging out changes to input values to the JavaScript console. An elegant way of testing how this works is to, for example, highlight the *for example* section of the initial value of the first input field and simply erase it, leaving only the value of *Old McDonald* in the input.

Doing this would result in the following sentence being logged to the console:

```
The value in the first input has changed from: e.g Old McDonald to: Old
McDonald.
```

In the next section, we will be looking at how to hook into various stages of a component's life and alter its behavior at that specific point with custom code.

Lifecycle hooks

Life cycle hooks are methods that let us alter the behavior of components at various stages of their life cycle.

What is a component's lifecycle?

It's just the natural progression of the *life* of a component.

Thus, we can say that lifecycle hooks are *points* along this journey that each component needs to go through. At these specific *points* in a component's life, we can use these methods to alter a component's behavior.

The Vue team has chosen very descriptive names for these lifecycle methods. What follows is the list of lifecycle hooks organized in the order of the natural progression of a component's life:

- beforeCreate
- created
- beforeMount
- mounted
- beforeUpdate
- updated
- activated
- deactivated
- beforeDestroy
- destroyed

This visual representation of a component's lifecycle is available at this address: `https://vuejs.org/images/life cycle.png`.

 Note that it would be beneficial that you print this image out and keep it with you until you fully understand the information it conveys. This will be of great help for getting a deeper understanding of Vue in general, and its component lifecycle in particular.

As we can see, there are five distinct stages of a component's life, and each stage has a lifecycle hook before a specific stage begins, and another lifecycle hook for after it is completed.

It is important to note that a component can be mounted several times, based on the changes in the data model. This is verifiable in the lifecycle diagram referenced in the previous tip box. However, it is also crucial to understand that the DOM re-rendering that takes place when the underlying data is changed can result in a component being effectively *unmounted,* even though this is not explicitly mentioned anywhere in the lifecycle diagram.

How do we use lifecycle hooks?

Let's look at a simple example, available at this Codepen URL: `https://codepen.io/AjdinImsirovic/pen/jprmoa`.

To begin with, let's add the HTML:

```
<div> Lorem ipsum dolor sit amet</div>
<div id="app">
  <custom-article :message="datacontent"></custom-article>
</div>
```

Next, let's add the CSS:

```
div,.thetemplate {
 font-size: 30px;
 padding: 20px;
 color: limegreen;
 font-family: Arial;
  border: 3px solid green;
  border-radius: 10px;
}
```

And finally, the JS:

```
Vue.component('custom-article', {
  props: {
    message: {
      type: String,
      required: true,
      default: 'Hello Vue'
    }
  },
  template: `<div class="thetemplate">{{ message }}</div>`
});

new Vue({
  el: "#app",
  beforeCreate() {
    alert("Lifecycle hook beforeCreate has been run");
  },
  created() {
    setTimeout(function(){
      alert('This message is showing 5 seconds after the \'created\' life
cycle hook');
    },5000);
  },
  data: function() {
    return {
      datacontent: 'This component was made with the help of a data
function in the Vue component called custom-article, and the data passed
was validated with the help of the props object inside the Vue component'
    }
  }
});
```

As can be seen in the Codepen provided, it is really easy to hook into life cycle methods in Vue. It's just a matter of providing the desired code (functionality) to the life cycle hook method name in the Vue instance.

In the previous example, we are showing an alert for the `beforeCreate()` method, and we are showing another alert 5 seconds after the `created()` method has been run.

There are many more useful things to do with life cycle hooks, which will be covered in the chapters which follow.

Summary

In this chapter, we looked at some basic concepts in Vue. We described why these concepts are important and how they can be used. We also looked at several simple examples of using these concepts in practice.

We learned about data-driven views in Vue and reactivity as a way to keep track of the changes to the data model. We looked at using computed properties and methods, directives, and their modifiers. We have seen some practical examples of components, templates, and props, as well as different approaches to building component templates in Vue.

We learned how to prototype websites using Vue components and directives, and we wrapped up the chapter with a look at watchers and lifecycle hooks as a powerful way to alter the behavior of components at any point of their lifecycle.

In the next chapter, we will further delve into reactive programming in Vue with a focus on components, props, and slots.

3

Working with Vue-CLI, Components, Props, and Slots

The previous chapter was an introduction to the basic concepts of Vue. We will start this chapter with a more realistic approach: we'll introduce Vue-cli. We'll look at the component hierarchy, global and local components, and communication between components. We will introduce slots, and we will also examine the difference between slots and props.

In this chapter, we will cover the following topics:

- Vue component hierarchy, and global and local components
- Using Vue-cli
- Setting up code editors to use with Vue
- The structure of our Vue-cli-based project
- Adding basic functionality to a child component
- Adding props to our `HelloAgain.vue`
- Introduction to slots

Vue component hierarchy, and global and local components

As we learned in `Chapter 2`, *Basic Concepts of Vue 2*, to get a new Vue instance running, we use new Vue:

```
new Vue(
  el: "#app",
  // the rest of the Vue instance code here
)
```

Our `app` component resides inside this Vue instance.

The app component usually has a child component, like we saw in this example from Chapter 2, *Basic Concepts of Vue 2*: `https://codepen.io/AjdinImsirovic/pen/xzpOaJ`:

```
Vue.component('custom-article', {
  template: `
    <article>
      Our own custom article component!
    </article>`
})
new Vue({
    el: '#app'
})
```

What we did not mention in the previous chapter is this:

- A child component can be reused as many times as needed
- A child component can also have its own children

An example of this is available in the following pen: `https://codepen.io/AjdinImsirovic/pen/ZjdOdK`.

Here is the code which demonstrates these two principles:

```
// JS
Vue.component('custom-article', {
  template: `
    <article>
      Our own custom article component!
    </article>`
})
Vue.component('another-custom-article', {
  template: `
    <article>
      Another custom article component!
      This one has it's own child component too!
      Here it is:
      <custom-article></custom-article>
    </article>`
})
new Vue({
    el: '#app'
})

/* CSS */
article {
```

```
    font-size: 40px;
    padding: 20px;
    color: limegreen;
    font-family: Arial;
    border: 3px solid green;
    border-radius: 10px;
}

<!-- HTML -->
<main id="app">
    <custom-article></custom-article>
    <custom-article></custom-article>
    <another-custom-article></another-custom-article>
</main>
```

As seen already, to add a component to our Vue instance, we are using the following syntax:

```
Vue.component('another-custom-article', { // etc...
```

In Vue terminology, we use this code to **register** a component. As described before, it's referred to as **global registration**. There is also **local registration**.

Local registration works similarly to the `Vue.component` syntax. The only difference in the code is how we introduce the local component when compared to a global one. In the previous code, we had the following global component:

```
Vue.component('custom-article', {
  template: `
    <article>
      Our own custom article component!
    </article>`
})
```

Converting this global component to a local component is as simple as removing this snippet of code:

```
Vue.component('custom-article'
```

Instead of the previous code, we'll simply make a new variable and give it the exact same options object that we used in the global component, like this:

```
var customArticle = {
  template: `
    <article>
      Our own custom article component!
    </article>`
}
```

In order to use this local component in our Vue instance, we'll introduce the `components` option, like this:

```
new Vue({
    el: '#app',
    components: {
      'custom-article': customArticle
    }
})
```

An example with a local component is available here: `https://codepen.io/ AjdinImsirovic/pen/ZMzrpr`.

However, the previous example is incomplete on purpose. As we can see, the `customArticle` local component is only available in the main Vue instance, but it is not available in the `anotherCustomArticle` component.

To make this work and complete the example, we need to tweak this bit of code:

```
Vue.component('another-custom-article', {
  template: `
    <article>
      Another custom article component!
      This one has it's own child component too!
      Here it is:
      <custom-article></custom-article>
    </article>`,
    //components: {
    // 'customArticle': customArticle
    //}
})
```

We will simply remove the comments on these three lines:

```
components: {
  'customArticle': customArticle
}
```

By doing that, we have registered the local component `customArticle` in the global component `anotherCustomArticle`. Basically, we are following the same procedure of registering a local component in our main Vue instance, and we are applying that same approach of registering local component in our `anotherCustomArticle` global component.

To get into the nuances of global and local registration, you can refer to this section of the official Vue documentation:
`https://vuejs.org/v2/guide/components-registration.html`.

In the following section, we'll start using Vue-cli.

Using Vue-CLI

In order to start using Vue-cli, we need to have Node.js set up on our machine, and we also need to have a command-line app on our operating system of choice.

For example, my preferred tools are Windows 10 and Git bash for Windows.

There are many different operating systems and command-line apps that you could potentially be using.

If you run into problems during the installation of any of the tools mentioned in this section, it might be worthwhile to have a look at this in-depth guide on installing Node.js on your operating system:

`https://www.packtpub.com/mapt/book/web_development/`
`9781788626859/2`

Installing Git bash

You first need to visit `https://git-scm.com/downloads`, which lets you choose between macOS X, Windows, and Linux/Unix installations. After clicking on the **Windows download**, you can proceed with the installation steps for Git bash. Just following the default preset options during the installation should be fine.

Installing nvm

To download the Node version manager for Windows, visit this link:
`https://github.com/coreybutler/nvm-windows/releases`

Once on the page, click the `nvm-setup.zip` file to download it, then run the downloaded `nvm-setup.exe` and go through the regular installation steps.

Next, start Git bash with administrator privileges and run the following command:

```
nvm install 8.11.4
```

The following message will be logged to the console:

```
Downloading node.js version 8.11.4 (64-bit)...
```

Why use nvm?

There are two major reasons:

- Security-critical upgrades

- Easier switching between Node versions in different projects

The first reason listed here has to do with future updates to Node.js. In case there is a major security patch a few month after this book is published, it would be smart to update Node on your system. Using nvm makes this easy, which brings us to the second point. Even if there are no major releases of Node available for you to upgrade, you could still run different versions of Node based on the needs of different projects you'll be working on. Either way, using nvm pays off.

Once the download is complete, in our Git bash we can simply run this command:

```
nvm use 8.11.4
```

Now, we are ready to use Vue-cli.

Installing and updating Vue-cli

It might be interesting to note that Vue-cli is a wrapper around Webpack, which has been tweaked and adjusted so it provides the best possible experience both during development and when releasing our Vue apps into production. This is a major plus for developers, since this setup lets us focus on coding without having to grapple with the toolchain for extended periods of time.

Let's open up Git bash and run the following command:

```
npm install -g vue-cli
```

Since Vue-cli is an `npm` package, you can read more about it here: `https://www.npmjs.com/package/vue-cli`.

To check the current version of Vue-cli installed on your system, run this command:

```
vue -V
```

Note that there has been a major upgrade between Vue-cli versions 2 and 3. To make sure that you are using the most up-to-date version on your system, you can run this command:

```
npm install @vue/cli
```

This command will update your version of Vue-cli to the most recent one. The update is local, meaning it will put it in the `node_modules` folder of the folder in which you run the previous command. Note that this operation could take some time because of all the dependencies that need to be installed.

Before initializing our project using Vue-cli, it would be beneficial to quickly list the improvements that version 3 of Vue-cli brings. Hopefully, this will reinforce some of the key points made in `Chapter 1`, *Introducing Vue*, regarding the ease of use of Vue.

The goals of version 3 of Vue-cli are as follows:

- Simplify and streamline tooling to avoid toolchain fatigue for frontend development
- Follow best practices in the tooling and thus make it become the default for Vue apps

There is also a whole slew of features and upgrades to the new version of Vue-cli:

- Preset Webpack configuration for hot module replacement, tree-shaking, and so on
- ES2017 features
- Babel 7 support
- PostCSS support
- Optional integration for Typescript, PWA, Jest, E2E testing, and so on

Put succinctly, Vue.js is keeping up with the times, and Vue-cli is just more proof of that.

Initializing a new project with Vue-cli

Once installed, we can initialize a new project with the following command:

```
vue create quickstart-vue
```

We are giving our Vue app the name of *quickstart-vue*. We might as well have named it anything else.

Once we run the preceding command, we can choose to use a preset, or to manually pick features we'd like to use:

```
$ vue create quickstart-vue
 ? Please pick a preset: (Use arrow keys)
 > default (babel, eslint)
 Manually select features
```

We could choose the default preset, but just as a little exercise, let's choose the **Manually select features** option instead. Then we'll choose npm rather then yarn. That will result in the following output on the screen:

```
$ vue create quickstart-vue
 ? Please pick a preset: (Use arrow keys)
 ? Please pick a preset: default (babel, eslint)
 ? Pick the package manager to use when installing dependencies: (Use arrow
keys)
 ? Pick the package manager to use when installing dependencies: NPM
Installing CLI plugins. This might take a while...
```

You will know that the plugins have been installed when you see this message:

```
 . . .
Successfully created project quickstart-vue.
Get started with the following commands:
$ cd quickstart-vue
 $ npm run serve
```

Now we can simply follow the previous instructions and change into the quickstart-vue directory:

```
cd quickstart-vue
```

Next, we will run the server (which is actually running a Webpack dev server in the background):

```
npm run serve
```

The message that our app is available at port `8080` will be logged out to the console. So, let's open up our browser at `http://localhost:8080` and look at the default site:

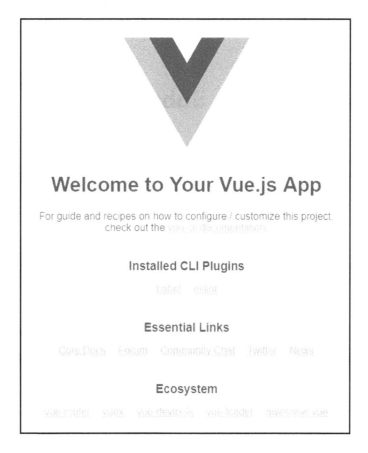

In the next section, we'll set up two editors to use with our new Vue project. These editors are Sublime Text and Visual Studio Code.

Setting up code editors to use with Vue

There are a number of code editors and **IDEs** (**integrated development environments**) that we can use to work with Vue. Some of the more popular ones include these:

- Sublime Text `https://www.sublimetext.com/`
- Visual Studio Code (VS Code), `https://code.visualstudio.com/`

- Atom, https://atom.io/
- WebStorm, https://www.jetbrains.com/webstorm/
- Visual Studio 2017, https://visualstudio.microsoft.com/downloads/

In this section, we'll look at using Vue.js in Sublime Text and VS Code.

Working with Vue.js in Sublime Text 3

Sublime Text is a mature and fun-to-use text editor, and so we will download it and set it up to be used with our Vue.js projects.

Dowloading Sublime Text 3

We'll begin by downloading Sublime Text 3 from the download page: https://www.sublimetext.com/3

Next, visit the website, https://packagecontrol.io/, which is the home of the package manager for Sublime Text.

Install Package Manager

On the package manager website, click the **Install Now** button in the top right of the page and follow these installation steps:

1. Select and copy all the text inside the Sublime Text 3 tab.
2. Open up the newly installed Sublime Text 3.
3. Inside Sublime Text 3, press the keyboard shortcut of *Ctrl +* ` (hold and press control and then press the backtick key). On most keyboards, the backtick character is available to the left of number 1 on the alphanumerical section of the keyboard.
4. Paste the code copied from https://packagecontrol.io into the bottom input field that opened up in the previous step.

After completing these steps, restart Sublime Text and you'll have access to a quick-launch installer via this keyboard shortcut: *Ctrl + Shift + P*.

This keyboard combination will display a little input in the middle of the screen, and you can type the word `install` inside it. This will show different options that you can either click on with a mouse or use the `arrow up` and `arrow down` keys to highlight, then the `Enter` key to run:

Next, select the option that reads **Package control: Install package**.

This is the list of packages that we will install:

- Vue Syntax Highlight, at `https://packagecontrol.io/packages/Vue%20Syntax%20Highlight`
- Vuejs Snippets, at `https://packagecontrol.io/packages/Vuejs%20Snippets`
- JavaScript Beautify, at `https://packagecontrol.io/packages/Javascript%20Beautify`

 Interestingly, the Chrome browser has recently* received a similar quick-launch functionality, available via the same shortcut keys. To see it in action, you can simply open the developer tools utility with the *F12* key and then run the *Ctrl + Shift + P* shortcut keys.

For example, in the launcher that opens, you can type the word **node**, then click on the first command in the drop-down, **Capture node screenshot**. This command will capture a screenshot of the element you are currently on in the DOM tree of the DevTools.

* A few months ago

In the next section, we'll look at setting up our Vue-based project in VS Code.

Working with Vue.js in VS Code

Although Sublime Text has the advantage of maturity and being light on the system, which makes it easy to use on slower machines, VS Code is a viable alternative.

Installing VS Code and extensions

Let's navigate to `https://code.visualstudio.com/download` and download the appropriate version of VS Code for our operating system.

 If you are using Widows 10, you can easily see if your system is 32-bit or 64-bit. Simply use the shortcut keys *Winkey + X*, then click **System** in the contextual menu. A new window will open and you'll see whether your system is 32-bit or 64-bit in the **Device Specifications** | **System type** area.

Once you have downloaded and opened VS Code, it's easy to add extensions to it. Simply click the bottom-most icon (the extensions icon) on the left side of the screen:

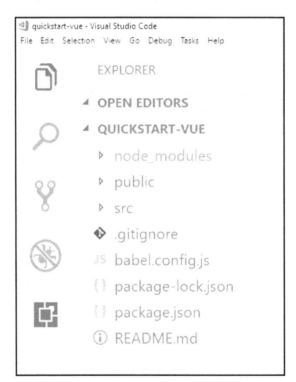

Clicking the icon will open up the extensions pane, into which you can type Vue and get back results similar to this:

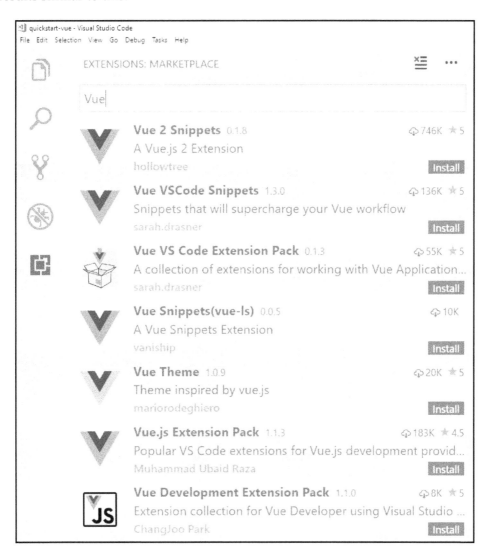

Next, simply choose either of the Vue VS Code Extension Packs, then click on the green **Install** button. Extensions that are part of this pack include syntax highlighting, snippets, linting and error checking, formatting (such as js-beautify), auto completion, hover info, auto-rename-tags, npm support for VS code, ES6 snippets, ESLint, and more.

Alternatively, if you want to avoid bloat in your VS Code extensions, you can reduce it somewhat by installing the Vetur extension by Pine Wu instead of the previously mentioned Vue extension pack.

Once the installation is complete, we can simply click the button that reads **Reload** to restart VS Code and activate the extension. Finally, to get back to the tree structure of our project, simply click the top-most icon on the left side of the screen, just under VS Code's main menu.

The structure of our Vue-cli-based project

In this section, we'll look at the file structure of our Vue project that we have set up using Vue-cli. Our `quickstart-vue` folder structure is as follows:

Let's first examine the contents of the `main.js` file:

```
import Vue from 'vue'
import App from './App.vue'

Vue.config.productionTip = false

new Vue({
  render: h => h(App)
}).$mount('#app')
```

We begin by importing `Vue` from the `vue` folder. This `vue` folder is located in your `node_modules` folder.

Next, we import `App` from `App.vue`.

As we have already learned, `new Vue` creates a Vue instance, and we then pass it the options object.

Inside the options object, we are only setting the `render` property. As we can see, the `render` property's value is an arrow function:

```
h => h(App)
```

The arrow function accepts, as its parameter, the `App` component that we imported on line two of the `main.js` file.

As you can probably tell, the previous function is written in ES6. Transpiled to ES5, it would look like this:

```
function(h) {
  return h(App);
}
```

The preceding function receives a Vue template to be rendered. Where will it render? It will render it in our `index.html` page, replacing whatever static piece of the DOM we pass to the `$mount()` function.

Which location in the DOM that will be depends on what we pass on as the parameter to the `$mount()` function. In the previous code, we passed the `#app` parameter.

Where does `'#app'` come from? It comes from the `App` component, or, more specifically, from the `App.vue` file, located in our `src` folder.

The `src` folder holds all the actual application code of our Vue project.

 Note that `main.js` is the only actual JavaScript file in our project—all the files in the `src` folder have the `.vue` extension. Every `.vue` file has three parts: the template, the script, and the style tag. The template defines the HTML of the component, the script defines the JS, and the style tag defines the CSS. Also, Vue-cli (with Webpack under the hood) puts all of this together because it understands how to work with `.vue` files.

Let's alter the `App.vue` file in our `src` folder, so that it looks like this:

```
<template>
  <div id="app">
    <HelloWorld msg="Welcome to Vue Quickstart!"/>
    <HelloAgain />
  </div>
</template>

<script>
import HelloWorld from './components/HelloWorld.vue';
import HelloAgain from './components/HelloAgain.vue'

export default {
  name: 'app',
  components: {
    HelloWorld, HelloAgain
  }
}
</script>

<style>
#app {
  font-family: sans-serif;
  text-align: center;
  color: #2c3e50;
  margin-top: 60px;
}
</style>
```

Let's also change the contents of `HelloWorld.vue`, so that it looks like this:

```
<template>
  <div class="hello">
    <h1>{{ msg }}</h1>
    <p>
      This is the beginning of something great.
    </p>
```

```
    </div>
  </template>

  <script>
  export default {
    name: 'HelloWorld',
    props: {
      msg: String
    }
  }
  </script>

  <!-- Add "scoped" attribute to limit CSS to this component only -->
  <style scoped>
  p {
    font-size: 20px;
    font-weight: 600;
    text-align: center;
  }
  </style>
```

Finally, let's add another component inside the `src/components/` folder. We'll call it `HelloAgain.vue`, and we'll give it the following code:

```
<template>
 <p class="hello-again">
 This is another component.
 </p>
</template>

<script>
export default {
 name: 'HelloAgain'
}
</script>

<style scoped>
p {
 font-size: 16px;
 text-align: center;
 color: tomato;
}
</style>
```

What we did in these three files is that we have mostly just removed some extra pieces of code to more clearly demonstrate the following points:

- Each `vue` file holds a single file component
- The structure of every single file component follows the same pattern: template at the top, script in the middle, and style at the bottom
- Style can be scoped to each individual file
- The `App.vue` file imports the components from the `components` folder and exports itself so that it can be used by `main.js`
- The `HelloWorld` and `HelloAgain` components simply export themselves to the parent component, the `App.vue` file
- In order to use the newly introduced component (the `HelloAgain` component), the `App.vue` file needs to add it inside its `<template>` tag
- The `App.vue` file also needs to both import and export the `HelloAgain` single file template so that `main.js` can use it

 `App.vue`, `HelloWorld.vue`, and `HelloAgain.vue` are examples of single-file components. Single-file components are the preferred way of working with components in our Vue projects.

If you have changed the files as described previously, you should have the following screen in your browser at `http://localhost:8080`:

Welcome to Vue Quickstart!

This is the beginning of something great.

This is another component

Now that we have seen how the `vue/components/` folder is organized and how it basically works, we will list other important files in our Vue project:

1. List of files that should not be tracked by Git source version control: `.gitignore`
2. Config file for Babel: `.babel.config.js`
3. File that lists the dependencies and other information of our npm-based projects: `package.json`
4. A manual for our app in markdown format: `README.md`

Of course, there is also the public folder, which contains our compiled application, referenced from the `index.html` file. This is the file that will ultimately be rendered and re-rendered in the browser, as our Vue app keeps compiling. The content of the `index` file is very simple:

```
<!DOCTYPE html>
<html lang="en">
  <head>
    <meta charset="utf-8">
    <meta http-equiv="X-UA-Compatible" content="IE=edge">
    <meta name="viewport" content="width=device-width,initial-scale=1.0">
    <link rel="icon" href="<%= BASE_URL %>favicon.ico">
    <title>quickstart-vue</title>
  </head>
  <body>
    <noscript>
      <strong>
        We're sorry but quickstart-vue doesn't work properly
        without JavaScript enabled. Please enable it to continue.
      </strong>
    </noscript>
    <div id="app"></div>
    <!-- built files will be auto injected -->
  </body>
</html>
```

As mentioned before, the `div` with the `id` attribute set to `app` is our Vue app's entry point.

Now that we have a better understanding of our project structure, we will move on to building child components.

In the next section, we will add some basic functionality to our `HelloAgain` component.

Adding basic functionality to a child component

In this section, we will add some very basic functionality to a child component. Before we get into the specifics of how this is done, we will also need to install the official Vue Chrome extension.

The Vue developer tools extension for Chrome is available at this URL: `http://bit.ly/2Pkpk2I`.

Installing the official Vue Chrome extension is straightforward; you just install it like any other Chrome extension.

Once you have completed the installation, you will have a Vue logo available in the top-right area of Chrome, and clicking that logo will give you the following message:

Vue.js is detected on this page. Open DevTools and look for the Vue panel.

Opening DevTools is easy: just press the F12 key. Then you can find the Vue panel as one of the tabs in the area which has the following tabs: **Elements**, **Console**, **Sources**, and so on. You should get something similar to the following screen:

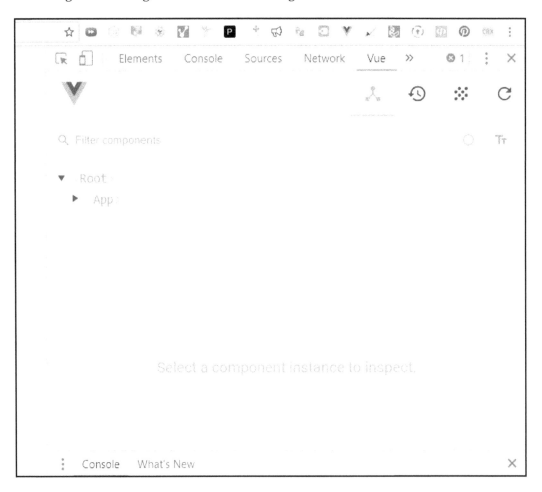

Back in VS Code, let's open up the `HelloAgain.vue` component and update the template section of the code so that it looks like this:

```
<template>
 <p class="hello-again">
 This is another component.
 <button v-on:click="incrementUp">Add One</button>
 <br>
 <span>Current value of the counter: {{ counter }}</span>
 </p>
</template>
```

Let's also update the `script` tag, like so:

```
<script>
export default {
 name: 'HelloAgain',
 data() {
     return {
         counter: 0
     }
 },
 methods: {
     incrementUp: function() {
         this.counter++
     }
 }
}
</script>
```

Finally, we'll update the styles to make our button look nicer:

```
<style scoped>
p {
 font-size: 16px;
 text-align: center;
 color: tomato;
}
button {
     display: block;
     margin: 10px auto;
     background: tomato;
     color: white;
     border: none;
     padding: 5px 10px;
     font-size: 16px;
     border-radius: 4px;
     cursor: pointer;
```

```
}
</style>
```

The end result of this update will be rendered in our browser as follows:

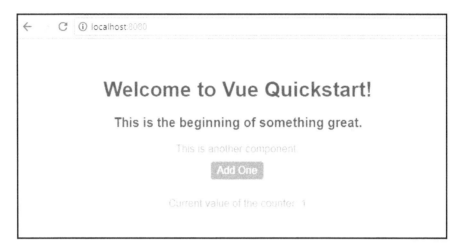

Now that we have looked at building templates and working with some basic functionality, let's switch our focus to another important topic: communication between components. We'll begin by revisiting props, which are a way to communicate between parent and child components.

Adding props to our HelloAgain.vue

In this section, we will briefly revisit props to see a practical example of how to communicate between a parent and a child component in Vue. In other words, we want to take some data from the parent component and pass it to the child component. The data we will be passing will simply be additional numbers to be included in the counter of our quickstart-vue app.

In our App.vue file, we'll add a button:

```
<template>
  <div id="app">
    <HelloWorld msg="Welcome to Vue Quickstart!"/>
    <button v-on:click="addTen">Add 10</button>
    <HelloAgain v-bind:counterFromParent="countUp"/>
  </div>
</template>
```

The button is placed between the two components we already had. We have added a v-on directive, tracking a click event on the button. The click event will trigger the addTen method, so we will specify it in between the <script> tags of our App.vue file:

```
methods: {
  addTen() {
    this.countUp += 10
  }
},
```

The addTen method is using the countUp piece of data, so let's add this new data to our <script> too:

```
data: function() {
  return {
    countUp: 0
  };
},
```

So, initially, our data function in App.vue returns countUp of zero. Whenever a user clicks the button in our App.vue component, the value of countUp increases by 10. This value is the data that we want to pass to the child component, namely to the HelloAgain.vue child component. Our goal is to add this data from the parent to the value stored in the counter in the child component.

This is where the props syntax comes in. To specify to our HelloAgain.vue component that it should expect the data from the parent, we will add the following code:

```
props: ['counterFromParent']
```

The value of the props key is an array, and we add strings of props that the child component should be expecting from the parent.

Note that the props option can also be an object. An example of using an object for our props option would be, for example, if we'd want to validate the data being passed from the parent to the child component. We will validate props in later chapters of this book.

Still in HelloAgain.vue, we will alter the <span> tag inside its template, like this:

```
<span>Current value of the counter: {{ counter + counterFromParent }}</span>
```

Now that we have set up the code in both the parent and the child, it's just the matter of passing the data from one to the other. We will do that inside the `App.vue` template by adding the `v-bind` directive to the `<HelloAgain />` tag. Here is the updated `App.vue` template:

```
<template>
  <div id="app">
    <HelloWorld msg="Welcome to Vue Quickstart!"/>
    <button v-on:click="addTen">Add 10</button>
    <HelloAgain v-bind:counterFromParent="countUp"/>
  </div>
</template>
```

Note that we are binding the `counterFromParent` to the value of `countUp`. The value of `countUp` starts from zero, and upon every button click on the parent's button, the `addTen` method will be run, which we specify in the `methods` option of the parent `<script>` tag.

The `addTen` method adds 10 to the current value of `countUp`.

On the child side, in the `HelloAgain.vue` component, we simply add the current value of `counterFromParent` to our `counter` variable. To get the value of `counterFromParent`, we list it in the `props` array of the `<script>` tag of our `HelloAgain.vue` component.

Passing data from children to parent components

To pass data from a child component to a parent component, we use the following syntax:

```
this.$emit();
```

The `$` sign is there to signify a built-in Vue function. This specific one, `$emit`, is used to send a custom event to the parent. The first parameter that we pass to the `$emit` function is the name of the custom event. For example, we could reset the counter to zero, so we might name the custom event like this:

```
this.$emit('counterHasBeenReset')
```

The second argument is the data to be passed, so we will pass the current counter value, like this:

```
this.$emit('counterHasBeenReset', this.countUp);
```

Of course, this means that we need to update the value of countUp so that it goes back to zero. In order to do that, we need to update the methods option in the script tag of our HelloAgain child component so that it looks like this:

```
methods: {
    incrementUp: function() {
        this.counter++
    },
    resetTheCounter() {
        this.countUp = 0;
        this.$emit('counterHasBeenReset', this.countUp);
    }
}
```

Basically, we are saying in our methods option that whenever the resetTheCounter method is run, the countUp value should be reset to 0. Next, we follow up by emitting this updated value in the counterHasBeenReset custom event.

Now let's add a reset button to the child component template tag, also in HelloAgain.vue. We will do that by simply adding another line to our template tag:

```
<button v-on:click="resetTheCounter">Reset parent-added values</button>
```

As we see here, the button click will run the resetTheCounter method.

Now that we are emitting the event, we will capture it in the parent component by using the following syntax:

```
<HelloAgain v-bind:counterFromParent="countUp" v-
on:counterHasBeenReset="countUp = $event" />
```

As we can see here, we have added to the <HelloAgain> tag in our parent component. Specifically, we have added a v-on directive as follows:

```
v-on:counterHasBeenReset="countUp = $event" />
```

The component is listening for the counterHasBeenReset custom event, which will be emitted from the child component. When such an event is captured in the parent, the value of countUp will be set to whatever its value is in the event itself. Since we have set it to zero, that's what it will be.

There are alternative ways to communicate between components in Vue (both parent-to-child and child-to-child), and we will discuss them in a later chapter, when we discuss Vuex.

The end result of this exercise is that we will reset the values in the counter that have been added from the parent component, but the event will not affect the values added from the child component.

Now that we have learned about custom events, we can continue our discussion of components by looking at slots.

Introduction to slots

Slots are a way to reuse components. With props, we are passing data to a component. But what if we wanted to pass entire components to other components? That's where slots come in.

Slots are simply a way to pass on more complex code to our components. They can be just some HTML, or even entire components.

To insert HTML elements from a parent to a child component, we use the `slot` element inside a child component:

```
<slot></slot>
```

The actual content of the slot is specified in the parent component.

Here is an example of slots in use:

```
<!-- HTML -->
<div id="app"></div>

// JS
Vue.component("basicComponent", {
  template: `
    <div>
      <slot name="firstSlot"></slot>
      <slot name="secondSlot"></slot>
      <slot></slot>
    </div>
  `
});

new Vue({
  el: "#app",
  template: `
    <basicComponent>
      <p slot="firstSlot">
        This content will populate the slot named 'firstSlot'
```

```
      in the 'basicComponent' template
    </p>
    <p slot="secondSlot">
      This content will populate the slot named 'secondSlot'
      in the 'basicComponent' template
    </p>
  </basicComponent>
  `
});

/* CSS */
div {
  font-size: 30px;
  padding: 20px;
  color: darkgoldenrod;
  font-family: Arial;
  border: 3px solid darkgoldenrod;
  border-radius: 0px;
}
```

This example can be viewed live here: `https://codepen.io/AjdinImsirovic/pen/ERoLQM`.

There are several key points when working with slots:

- Slots are implemented based on the web component's spec draft
- The slot styling is determined by the scoped style tag in the child component
- Slots enable the use of composable components
- You can use any template code in slots
- If you have more than one slot, you can name them (using the `name` attribute)
- If you have more than one slot, you can leave out the `name` attribute in one of them, and that one will be the default slot
- As of Vue 2.1.0, slots can be scoped
- Slot scope can be destructured using ES2015 expression destructuring

To add default information to a slot, you can simply add content to the slot tag.

It's as simple as changing the code of the slot tag from this:

```
<slot></slot>
```

And changing it to this:

```
<slot>This is some default information</slot>
```

If you update the provided example pen by adding the default unnamed slot code referenced just above this line, you will notice the slot gets populated even though we have not referenced it in our Vue instance.

Summary

In this chapter, we looked at Vue's components. We discussed the Vue component hierarchy and the differences between global and local components. We fired up Vue-cli v3 and learned how to use it. We worked with .vue files and we set up the development in a couple of code editors. We learned about adding functionality to child components and the use cases for both props and slots. Finally, we looked at component communication in Vue.

In the next chapter, we will discuss filters as a way of changing what gets rendered on the screen without affecting the data behind it. We will also see how to adhere to the DRY rule of programming with the help of mixins.

4
Filters and Mixins

In this chapter, we will show how we can use filters to change what gets rendered on the screen without changing the underlying data. We'll also cover mixins, a practical way to extend components and adhere to the DRY rule of programming.

More specifically, in this chapter, we will discuss the following:

- Using filters:
    - Working with global and local filters
    - Replacing conditional directives with filters
    - Chaining filters together
- Working with mixins:
    - Avoiding code duplication inside mixin methods
    - Using data option to add more functionality to our mixins
    - Employing life cycle hooks in mixins

Using filters

A filter is just a function. It takes some data (passed in as an argument to the filter function), and performs some simple operations on that data. The result of the operations performed is returned from the filter function and displayed in the appropriate place in the app. It's important to note that filters do not affect the underlying data; they only affect the way that data is displayed on the screen.

Just like components, filters too can be registered as either global or local. The syntax for registering a global filter is as follows:

```
Vue.filter('justAnotherFilter', function(someData1, someData2, someDataN) {
  // the filter function definition goes here (it takes N number of
arguments)
});
```

Besides global registration, we can also register a filter locally, like this:

```
filters: {
  justAnotherFilter(someData1, someData2, someDataN) {
    // the filter function is defined here...
  }
}
```

As we can see here, in case of local registration, filters are added as an option to a Vue component.

An example of a filter that rounds up student grades

Let's say that we have a friend who is a professor, and they need some help with their students' tests. A test that students take is set up in such a way that it always produces a score in the form of a decimal number. The range of points a student can get on that test is between 0 and 100.

Being the good friend that we are, we will make a simple Vue app with a filter that rounds up decimal scores to full numbers. We will also err on the side of the student, meaning we will always round up the result.

The code for this example is available at https://codepen.io/AjdinImsirovic/pen/MqBNBR.

The function for our filter is going to be very simple: it will take in a float and return a rounded up integer based on the received float. The filter function will be called pointsRoundedUp, and it will look like this:

```
filters: {
  pointsRoundedUp(points){
    return Math.ceil(parseFloat(points));
  }
}
```

Hence our `pointsRoundedUp` function takes in the `points` instance from our app's `data()` function, and returns those `points` instance with JavaScript's built-in `parseFloat()` and `Math.ceil()` functions called on the `points` value.

To use a filter in our HTML, we employ the following syntax:

```
{{ points| pointsRoundedUp }}
```

The `points` value is the actual data stored in the app. `pointsRoundedUp` is the filter that we use to format the data we receive from our Vue component's data option.

Generally, we could say that the underlying logic of all filters is as follows:

```
{{ data | formattedData }}
```

This general principle could be read like this: to format the data that gets returned, we follow it up with a pipe symbol (|) and then we call a specific filter on that data.

Let's examine the full code of our app. The HTML will be as follows:

```
<div id="app">
 <h1>A simple grade-rounding Vue app</h1>
 <p>Points from test: {{ points }}</p>
 <p>Rounded points are: {{ points | pointsRoundedUp }}</p>
</div>
```

The JS will be simple too:

```
new Vue({
  el: "#app",
  data() {
    return {
      points: 74.44
    }
  },
  filters: {
    pointsRoundedUp(points){
      return Math.ceil(parseFloat(points));
    }
  }
});
```

The app will output the following on the screen:

A simple grade-rounding Vue app
```
Points from test: 74.44
Rounded points are: 75
```

The app is now complete.

However, after some time, our friend asks us for another favor: to calculate the student's grade based on the points. Initially, we realize that it will be just a tiny calculation, which we can simply fit into conditional directives.

The code for the updated example can be found here: `https://codepen.io/AjdinImsirovic/pen/XPPrEN`.

Basically, what we did in this new example is we extended our HTML with several conditional directives. Although this solves the problem, we have cluttered our HTML, while our JS has remained unchanged. The updated HTML code is as follows:

```html
<div id="app">
  <h1>A simple grade-rounding Vue app</h1>
  <p>Points from test: {{ points }}</p>
  <p>Rounded points are: {{ points | pointsRoundedUp }}</p>
  <p v-if="points > 90">Final grade: A</p>
  <p v-else-if="points > 80 && points <= 90">Final grade: B</p>
  <p v-else-if="points > 70 && points <= 80">Final grade: C</p>
  <p v-else-if="points > 60 && points <= 70">Final grade: D</p>
  <p v-else-if="points > 50 && points <= 86">Final grade: E</p>
  <p v-else="points <= 50">Final grade: F</p>
</div>
```

Our problem is solved. The points for this test are 94.44, and the app successfully prints out the following information to the screen:

A simple grade-rounding Vue app
```
Points from test: 94.44
Rounded points are: 95
Final grade: A
```

However, we realize that our HTML is now cluttered. Luckily, we can utilize filters to make things less messy.

Using filters as a replacement for conditional directives

In this section, we will employ a filter to return the proper grade for our student.

The code for the updated app is available here: `https://codepen.io/AjdinImsirovic/pen/LJJPKm`.

The changes we made to this version of the app's HTML are as follows:

```
<div id="app">
  <h1>A simple grade-rounding Vue app</h1>
  <p>Points from test: {{ points }}</p>
  <p>Rounded points are: {{ points | pointsRoundedUp }}</p>
  <p>Final grade: {{ points | pointsToGrade }}</p>
</div>
```

We moved the conditional functionality to our JavaScript, namely, to a new filter we named `pointsToGrade`:

```
new Vue({
  el: "#app",
  data() {
    return {
      points: 84.44
    }
  },
  filters: {
    pointsRoundedUp(points){
      return Math.ceil(parseFloat(points));
    },
    pointsToGrade(points){
      if(points>90) {
        return "A"
      } else if(points>80 && points<=90) {
        return "B"
      } else if(points>70 && points<=80) {
        return "C"
      } else if(points>60 && points<=70) {
        return "D"
      } else if(points>50 && points<=60) {
        return "E"
      } else {
        return "F"
      }
    }
```

```
    }
  });
```

As a quick test that our updated code works, we have also changed the points to 84.44, which successfully returns the B grade from the `pointsToGrade` filter.

However, not entirely unexpectedly, our friend returns again, and asks us for yet another favor: to extend the app yet again. This time, we need to display a properly formatted name of our student, in the following format:

```
Last name, First name, year of study, grade.
```

This means that we'll have to expand our app with additional functionality. Luckily, that won't be hard because we can employ another nice feature of filters: chaining.

Chaining filters in Vue

The requirements for our app have been updated, and now we need to show some additional, nicely formatted data on the screen.

Since the requirements have changed, we also need to update the data.

The code for this section is available at this pen: `https://codepen.io/AjdinImsirovic/pen/BOOazy`.

This is the updated JavaScript. To begin, we'll add the `el` and `data` options:

```
new Vue({
  el: "#app",
  data() {
    return {
      firstName: "JANE",
      lastName: "DOE",
      yearOfStudy: 1,
      points: 84.44,
      additionalPoints: 8
    }
  },
```

Still in JS, we'll add the filters:

```
filters: {
  pointsRoundedUp(points){
    return Math.ceil(parseFloat(points));
  },
  pointsToGrade(points){
```

```
  if(points>90) {
    return "A"
  }
  else if(points>80 && points<=90) {
    return "B"
  }
  else if(points>70 && points<=80) {
    return "C"
  }
  else if(points>60 && points<=70) {
    return "D"
  }
  else if(points>50 && points<=60) {
    return "E"
  }
  else {
    return "F"
  }
},
yearNumberToWord(yearOfStudy){
  // freshman 1, sophomore 2, junior 3, senior 4
  if(yearOfStudy==1) {
    return "freshman"
  } else if(yearOfStudy==2){
    return "sophomore"
  } else if(yearOfStudy==3){
    return "junior"
  } else if(yearOfStudy==4){
    return "senior"
  } else {
    return "unknown"
  }
},
firstAndLastName(firstName, lastName){
  return lastName + ", " + firstName
},
toLowerCase(value){
  return value.toLowerCase()
},
capitalizeFirstLetter(string) {
    return string.charAt(0).toUpperCase() + string.slice(1);
  }
  }
});
```

The updated HTML looks like this:

```
<div id="app">
  <h1>A simple grade-rounding Vue app</h1>
  <p>Points from test: {{ points }}</p>
  <p>Rounded points are: {{ points | pointsRoundedUp }}</p>
  <p>Student info:
  <!--
  <p>Name: {{ firstName, lastName | firstAndLastName | toLowerCase |
capitalizeFirstLetter}}</p>
  -->
  <p>
    Name:
    {{ lastName | toLowerCase | capitalizeFirstLetter }},
    {{ firstName | toLowerCase | capitalizeFirstLetter }}
  </p>
  <p>Year of study: {{ yearOfStudy | yearNumberToWord }}</p>
  <p>Final grade: <strong>{{ points | pointsToGrade }}</strong></p>
</div>
```

With these chained filters, we achieved the correct formatting of the student's name by virtue of taking the data (which appeared in all CAPS) and piping it through two filters: `toLowerCase` and `capitalizeFirstLetter`.

We can also see a commented-out paragraph that shows an unsuccessful approach that capitalizes only the first letter of the last name, but not the first letter of the first name. The reason for this is the `firstAndLastName` filter which, when applied, combines the full name into a single string.

Note that filters are not cached, which means that they will be always run, just like methods.

For more information on filters, refer to the official documentation at `https://vuejs.org/v2/guide/filters.html`.

Working with mixins

Mixins are a way for us to abstract out reusable functionality in our Vue code. Made popular in the frontend world by Sass, the concept of mixins is now present in a number of modern JavaScript frameworks.

Mixins are best used when we have some functionality that we would like to reuse across a number of components. In the example that follows, we will create a very simple Vue app, which will show two Bootstrap alerts on the page. When a user clicks on either of the alerts, the browser's viewport dimensions will be logged out to the console.

For this example to work, we will need to get some plain HTML components from the Bootstrap framework. Specifically, we will use the alert component.

The official documentation on this Bootstrap component can be found at this link: `https://getbootstrap.com/docs/4.1/components/alerts/`.

It is important to note that Bootstrap components and Vue components are different things and should not be confused.

The app, when run, will produce this result:

Extracting reusable functionality into mixins in Vue

A simple primary alert—check it out!

A simple warning alert—check it out!

The code for this example can be found here: `https://codepen.io/AjdinImsirovic/pen/jvvybq`.

Building a simple app with repetitive functionality in different components

To begin, let's build our simple HTML:

```
<div id="app">
  <div class="container mt-4">
    <h1>{{heading}}</h1>
```

```
      <primary-alert></primary-alert>
      <warning-alert></warning-alert>
    </div>
</div>
```

We are using Bootstrap's CSS classes of `container` and `mt-4`. The regular HTML `h1` tag also gets some Bootstrap-specific styling. We are also using two Vue components in the previous code: `primary-alert` and `warning-alert`.

In our JavaScript code, we define these two components as `primaryAlert` and `warningAlert`, and then we list them in the `components` option of their parent component:

```
const primaryAlert = {
  template: `
    <div class="alert alert-primary" role="alert" v-
on:click="viewportSizeOnClick">
      A simple primary alert—check it out!
    </div>`,
    methods: {
    viewportSizeOnClick(){
      const width = window.innerWidth;
      const height = window.innerHeight;
      console.log("Viewport width:", width, "px, viewport height:", height,
"px");
    }
  }
}
const warningAlert = {
  template: `
    <div class="alert alert-warning" role="alert" v-
on:click="viewportSizeOnClick">
      A simple warning alert—check it out!
    </div>`,
    methods: {
    viewportSizeOnClick(){
      const width = window.innerWidth;
      const height = window.innerHeight;
      console.log("Viewport width:", width, "px, viewport height:", height,
"px");
    }
  }
}
```

And now, still in JS, we can specify the constructor:

```
new Vue({
  el: '#app',
  data() {
    return {
      heading: 'Extracting reusable functionality into mixins in Vue'
    }
  },
  components: {
    primaryAlert: primaryAlert,
    warningAlert: warningAlert
  }
})
```

To see the result of this little app, open the console and click on either of the two alert components. The console output will be similar to the following:

```
Viewport width: 930 px, viewport height: 969 px
```

As we can see in the JavaScript code, we are also defining a `viewportSizeOnClick` method inside the `methods` option of both the `primaryAlert` and `warningAlert` components. This unnecessary repetition in functionality is a perfect candidate for abstracting into a mixin, which we will do next.

Staying DRY with mixins

The code for the improved app is available here: `https://codepen.io/AjdinImsirovic/pen/NLLgWP`.

In this example, while our HTML stays completely the same, the updated JavaScript code will look as follows:

```
const viewportSize = {
    methods: {
      viewportSizeOnClick(){
        const width = window.innerWidth;
        const height = window.innerHeight;
        console.log("Viewport width:", width, "px, viewport height:",
height, "px");
      }
  }
}
const primaryAlert = {
  template: `
```

```
      <div class="alert alert-primary" role="alert" v-
on:click="viewportSizeOnClick">
        A simple primary alert—check it out!
      </div>`,
  mixins: [viewportSize]
}
const warningAlert = {
  template: `
      <div class="alert alert-warning" role="alert" v-
on:mouseenter="viewportSizeOnClick">
        A simple warning alert—check it out!
      </div>`,
  mixins: [viewportSize]
}
new Vue({
  el: '#app',
  data() {
    return {
      heading: 'Extracting reusable functionality into mixins in Vue'
    }
  },
  components: {
    primaryAlert: primaryAlert,
    warningAlert: warningAlert
  }
})
```

As can be seen here, we have erased the methods option from both components and added a new object named viewportSize. Inside this object, we have moved the shared methods option:

```
const viewportSize = {
    methods: {
      viewportSizeOnClick(){
        const width = window.innerWidth;
        const height = window.innerHeight;
        console.log("Viewport width:", width, "px, viewport height:",
height, "px");
      }
    }
}
```

The methods option holds only the viewportSizeOnClick function.

As a side note, the `vieportSizeOnClick` method's name is slightly misleading. If you look at the code for the second component (the `warningAlert` component) a bit closer, you'll notice that we updated the directive so it is using `v-on:mouseenter`, rather than `v-on:click`. This means that the name of the method will need to be changed to something more suitable. Therefore, we will rename the method to `logOutViewportSize`.

Also, let's imagine that we want another way to display the viewport information. For example, we might show it in an alert box rather than logging it to the console. That's why we'll introduce another method, `alertViewportSize`.

With all of these little changes accumulating, it is a good time to see another, updated version of our little app. The new pen can be found at this URL: `https://codepen.io/AjdinImsirovic/pen/aaawJY`.

Similar to the previous updates, again the updated example only has changes made to the JS, as follows. We begin with `viewportSize`:

```
const viewportSize = {
    methods: {
       logOutViewportSize(){
          const width = window.innerWidth;
          const height = window.innerHeight;
          console.log("Viewport width:", width, "px, viewport height:",
height, "px");
       },
       alertViewPortSize() {
          const width = window.innerWidth;
          const height = window.innerHeight;
          alert("Viewport width: " + width + " px, viewport height: " +
height + " px");
       }
    }
}
```

Next, we'll set up the alerts:

```
const primaryAlert = {
  template: `
    <div class="alert alert-primary" role="alert" v-
on:click="alertViewPortSize">
       A simple primary alert—check it out!
    </div>`,
  mixins: [viewportSize]
}
const warningAlert = {
  template: `
```

```
        <div class="alert alert-warning" role="alert" v-
    on:mouseenter="logOutViewportSize">
        A simple warning alert—check it out!
    </div>`,
    mixins: [viewportSize]
}
```

Finally, let's wrap it up with specifying the Vue constructor:

```
new Vue({
    el: '#app',
    data() {
        return {
            heading: 'Extracting reusable functionality into mixins in Vue'
        }
    },
    components: {
        primaryAlert: primaryAlert,
        warningAlert: warningAlert
    }
})
```

In the next section, we will look at how we can further improve our mixins by refactoring them.

Refactoring our viewportSize mixin

In this section, we will look at ways to further improve our mixins. While our code is both readable and easy to grasp, we have some code duplication in `const` declarations. Also, we will use this opportunity to look at ways of approaching mixin refactoring. The updated code will include some basic event handling.

For the list of available events, refer to this link: `https://developer.mozilla.org/en-US/docs/Web/Events`.

Since we will also use JavaScript's built-in `addEventListener()` method, it would also be good to get more information about it on MDN, at the following URL: `https://developer.mozilla.org/en-US/docs/Web/API/EventTarget/addEventListener`.

Before we begin refactoring, we will utilize the ability of mixings to plug into the life cycle functionality of Vue (just like components do). Additionally, in this iteration of our mixin, we introduce another option besides `methods` in the mixin itself. The option we use is `data`. Effectively, to avoid having to duplicate `const` declarations inside the `methods` option of our mixin, we will store the values to work with inside the `data` option.

While the HTML still remains unchanged, our JavaScript file will look quite different. Let's begin by setting up the data:

```
const viewportSize = {
    data(){
      return {
        viewport: {
          width: 0,
          height: 0
        }
      }
    },
```

Next, we'll add methods, namely getViewportSize, logOutViewportSize, and alertViewportSize:

```
    methods: {
      measureViewportSize(){
        this.viewport.width = window.innerWidth;
        this.viewport.height = window.innerHeight;
      },
      logOutViewportSize(){
        console.log("Viewport width:", this.viewport.width, "px, viewport
  height:", this.viewport.height, "px");
      },
      alertViewPortSize() {
        alert("Viewport width: " + this.viewport.width + " px, viewport
  height: " + this.viewport.height + " px");
      }
    },
```

Next, let's add created:

```
created() {
    this.listener =
      window.addEventListener('mousemove',this.measureViewportSize);
    this.measureViewportSize();
  }
}
```

Now, we can set up primaryAlert:

```
const primaryAlert = {
  template: `
    <div class="alert alert-primary" role="alert" v-
on:click="alertViewPortSize">
      A simple primary alert—check it out!
    </div>`,
```

```
    mixins: [viewportSize]
  }
```

We'll continue by adding `warningAlert`:

```
const warningAlert = {
  template: `
    <div class="alert alert-warning" role="alert" v-
on:mouseenter="logOutViewportSize">
      A simple warning alert—check it out!
    </div>`,
  mixins: [viewportSize]
}
```

Finally, let's add the Vue constructor:

```
new Vue({
  el: '#app',
  data() {
    return {
      heading: 'Extracting reusable functionality into mixins in Vue'
    }
  },
  components: {
    primaryAlert: primaryAlert,
    warningAlert: warningAlert
  }
})
```

The code for this section is available in the following code pen: `https://codepen.io/AjdinImsirovic/pen/oPPGLW`.

The options we have in our refactored mixin are `data`, `methods`, and `created`. The `created` function is a life cycle hook, and we use this hook to listen for `mousemove` events. When such an event occurs, we run the `this.getViewportSize` method of our mixin, which updates the viewport dimensions that get either logged out or shown in an alert box.

Never use global mixins! Global mixins affect all of the components of your apps. There are not that many use cases for such a scenario, so usually it is best to avoid using global mixins.

With this, we conclude our brief discussion of mixins in Vue. For more information on the subject, visit this official link:

```
https://vuejs.org/v2/guide/mixins.html
```

Summary

In this chapter, we looked at filters and mixins in Vue. We discussed the situations in which using filters would make sense, and we looked at using global and local filters. We also discussed how filters can be used to replace conditional directives, and we examined how to pipe filters together.

We also explored how to abstract reusable functionality by moving it from components to mixins, and we looked at ways to avoid code duplication inside mixins themselves. We wrapped it up with an example of using life cycle hooks inside our mixins.

In the next chapter, we will look at building our own custom directives.

5
Making Your Own Directives and Plugins

In this chapter, we will look at ways of extending Vue. First, we will code our own directives and see how we can use them. Next, we will make a custom Vue plugin.

More specifically, in this chapter, we will examine the following:

- The structure of custom directives and how to make them
- Using global and local custom directives
- Passing values to custom directives
- Authoring Vue plugins
- Publishing Vue plugins

Making our own directives

In Vue 2, components are the go-to strategy to use, be it keeping things DRY or abstracting away some functionality. However, another approach that you can take is to utilize custom directives.

Understanding custom directives

As we discussed earlier in this book, directives help us explain to Vue what kind of behavior we would like to attach to a piece of markup. As we have previously seen, there are a number of directives that come built-in with Vue. Some examples are `v-on`, `v-if`, `v-model`, and so on. As a quick refresher, a directive is an HTML attribute that starts with `v-`.

When we need to build a custom directive, we simply provide a custom word after the hyphen. For example, we could create a custom directive, which we'll call `v-custom-directive`, and we can then use this name in our markup, for example, like this:

```
<div id="app">
  <div v-custom-directive>{{ something }}</div>
<!-- etc -->
```

Note that it is perfectly normal to have a directive without a value, just like it is to provide it a value, like so:

```
<div id="app">
  <div v-custom-directive="aValue">{{ something }}</div>
<!-- etc -->
```

Next, in our JS code, we would need to register this directive, as follows:

```
Vue.directive('customDirective', {
  // details for the directive go here
}
```

So, as we can see, the first argument provided to `Vue.directive` is the name of our custom directive. Note that the Vue convention of using kebab-case in HTML and lowerCamelCase in JS is also applied to custom directives.

The second argument provided to our custom directive is an object that holds all of the directive's functionality.

As you might infer by now, the previous code gives an example of registering a directive globally. If you would like to register a directive locally, you would need to specify a `directives` option to a specific component.

For example, we could register a local component as follows:

```
directives: {
  directiveName: {
    // some code to describe functionality
  }
}
```

Just like components, directives use hooks too, which allows us to control when their functionality will be called. There are five directive hooks: `bind`, `inserted`, `update`, `componentUpdated`, and `unbind`.

For a full list of arguments that some of these hooks can take, you can refer to `https://vuejs.org/v2/guide/custom-directive.html#Directive-Hook-Arguments`.

Building a simple custom directive

The full code for this example is available here: `https://codepen.io/AjdinImsirovic/pen/yxWObV`.

In our HTML, we will add the following simple code:

```
<div id="app" class="container mt-5">
  <h1 class="h2">{{ heading }}</h1>
  <div v-custom-directive>
    Just some text here
  </div>
</div>
```

In our JS, we will add our `customDirective` globally:

```
Vue.directive('customDirective', {
  inserted: function(el) {
    el.style.cssText = `
      color: blue;
      border: 1px solid black;
      background: gray;
      padding: 20px;
      width: 50%;
    `
  }
});

new Vue({
  el: '#app',
  data() {
    return {
      heading: 'A custom global directive'
    }
  }
});
```

In the previous code, we are using the `inserted` directive hook. With this hook, the directive's code will be run when the element that the directive is bound to is *inserted* into its parent node.

When this occurs, the element will be styled according to the values we assigned to `el.style.cssText`.

Of course, there is nothing preventing us from using more than one custom directive on an element. For example, we could specify several custom directives, and then mix and match them as suitable.

In the next section, we are going to rewrite the global custom directive as a local one.

Using local directives

Let's now look at how we could rewrite the previous code so that our directive uses local directives instead of a global one.

In this section, we will build a very simple custom directive. We will use an example from `Chapter 4`, *Filters and Mixins*, and we will build on it, so that we can easily compare the differences to the previous example, only this time with a simple local custom directive.

The code for this example is available here: `https://codepen.io/AjdinImsirovic/pen/yxWJNp`.

In our HTML, we will specify the following code:

```
<main id="app">
    <custom-article v-custom-directive></custom-article>
    <custom-article></custom-article>
    <another-custom-article v-another-custom></another-custom-article>
</main>
```

In our JS, we will specify the following code:

```
const anotherCustom = {
  inserted: function(el) {
    el.style.cssText = `
      color: green;
      border: 1px solid black;
      background: yellow;
      padding: 20px;
      width: 50%;
    `

  }
}

const customArticle = {
  template: `
    <article>
      Our own custom article component!
    </article>`
```

```
}

Vue.component('another-custom-article', {
  template: `
    <article>
      Another custom article component!
      This one has it's own child component too!
      Here it is:
      <custom-article v-custom-directive></custom-article>
    </article>`,
    components: {
      'customArticle': customArticle
    },
    directives: {
      customDirective: {
        inserted: function(el) {
          el.style.cssText = `
            color: blue;
            border: 1px solid black;
            background: gray;
            padding: 20px;
            width: 50%;
          `
        }
      }
    }
})

new Vue({
    el: '#app',
    components: {
      'customArticle': customArticle,
    },
    directives: {
      customDirective: {
        inserted: function(el) {
          el.style.cssText = `
            color: blue;
            border: 1px solid black;
            background: gray;
            padding: 20px;
            width: 50%;
          `
        }
      },
      'anotherCustom': anotherCustom
    }
})
```

In the next section, we will see how to pass values to custom directives.

Passing values to custom directives

We will improve on this chapter's initial example by allowing our custom directives to receive arguments. The code for this example is available in this pen: `https://codepen.io/AjdinImsirovic/pen/xaNgPN`.

This is the HTML for our example of passing values to custom directives:

```
<div id="app" class="container mt-5">
  <h1 class="h2">{{ heading }}</h1>
  <button v-buttonize="tomato">
    Just some text here
  </button>
  <button v-buttonize="lightgoldenrod">
    Just some text here
  </button>
  <button v-buttonize="potato">
    Just some text here
  </button>
</div>
```

And here is the JavaScript:

```
Vue.directive('buttonize', {
  bind(el, binding) {
    var exp = binding.expression;
    el.style.cssText += `
      padding: 10px 20px;
      border: none;
      border-radius: 3px;
      cursor: pointer
    `;
    switch(exp) {
      case 'tomato':
          el.style.cssText += `
            background: tomato;
            color: white;
          `;
          break;
        case 'lightgoldenrod':
          el.style.cssText += `
            background: darkgoldenrod;
            color: lightgoldenrod;
          `;
```

```
          break;
       default:
          el.style.cssText += `
            background: gray;
            color: white;
          `
      }
    }
  });
```

Finally, still in JS, we add the Vue constructor with the `options` object:

```
new Vue({
  el: '#app',
  data() {
    return {
      heading: 'A custom global directive'
    }
  }
});
```

Note that the specific settings for directive hook arguments can be found at `https://vuejs.org/v2/guide/custom-directive.html#Directive-Hook-Arguments`. The one argument that is of most interest to us is `binding`, which is an object with these properties: `name`, `value`, `oldValue`, `expression`, `arg`, and `modifiers`.

In the previous code, we see an example of passing two different values that give us different results based on the values passed. We also see an example of what happens when we pass a nonsensical value (one that utilizes the `switch` statement's `default` branch).

In the next section, we will discuss ways in which we can further extend Vue functionality by building Vue plugins.

Working with Vue plugins

Some popular Vue plugins are Vuex and Vue-router. A Vue plugin is used when we need to give additional functionality to Vue globally. There are a few very common scenarios where Vue plugins might be useful: adding global methods, adding global assets, adding instance methods on `Vue.prototype`, or adding global mixins.

Where Vue plugins shine is the ability to share them with the community. To get an idea of the vastness of Vue's plugin system, navigate to the following URLs: `https://github.com/vuejs/awesome-vue#components--libraries` and `https://vuejsexamples.com/`.

Next, we'll create a simple Vue plugin.

Creating the simplest possible Vue plugin

We'll begin by creating the simplest possible Vue plugin. In order to do that, we'll again use Vue CLI, version 3. The instructions for setting up Vue CLI are available in Chapter 3, *Working with Vue-CLI, Components, Props, and Slots.*

First, we will need to initialize a new project. Navigate your console to the parent folder in which you want to create a new Vue project, and run the following commands:

```
vue create simple-plugin
cd simple-plugin
npm run-serve
```

When we run the first of these three commands, we will be asked a few questions, and after that, a large number of packages will be run. This can take some time—a nice opportunity for a short break. Once done, and we have run the other two commands listed before, our boilerplate Vue app will be available at localhost:8080.

To start off, let's create a new folder inside the src folder and call it plugins. Next, inside the plugins folder, let's make another folder, which we'll call SimplePlugin. Inside the SimplePlugin folder, let's make a new file and call it index.js.

A Vue plugin is an object. For our plugin object to be accessible to our Vue app, we need to make it available by exporting it. Therefore, let's add this export code to our index.js file:

```
export default {

}
```

A Vue's plugin object has an install method. The install method takes in two arguments. The first argument is the Vue object, and the second argument is the options object. Therefore, we'll add the install method inside the plugin object:

```
export default {
    install(Vue, options) {
        alert('This is a simple plugin and currently the options argument
is ' + options);
    }
}
```

Currently, inside our `install` method, we are only alerting a message to the browser. This is the absolute minimum of functionality our plugin can have. With this functionality in place, it's time to use our plugin inside our app.

 Note that we are also concatenating the `options` argument to our alert message. If we didn't do it, our Vue-cli would throw an error, stating that *options is defined but never used.* Apparently, it favors the *(no-unused-vars)* scenarios.

To use the plugin, we need to open our `main.js` file and import the plugin by adding these two lines of code on line three of the `main.js` file:

```
import SimplePlugin from './plugins/SimplePlugin'
Vue.use(SimplePlugin)
```

First, we import the plugin and we specify the import path. Next, we add our plugin as an argument to the `Vue.use` method.

With this, we have successfully authored the simplest possible plugin. Open your local project at `localhost:8080` and you'll be greeted with the alert message, stating this:

```
This is the simplest possible Vue plugin and currently the options argument
is undefined
```

Next, we'll see how to add the options object to our plugins.

Creating a plugin with options defined

Due to the way we have set up our project, we will leave `SimplePlugin` as is and, in this section of our exploration of plugins in Vue, we'll add another folder inside our `plugins` folder in our project. We'll call this folder `OptionsPlugin` and inside of it, we'll again create an `index.js` file.

Next, let's update the `main.js` file, so that now it looks like this:

```
import Vue from 'vue'
import App from './App.vue'

//import SimplePlugin from './plugins/SimplePlugin'
import OptionsPlugin from './plugins/OptionsPlugin'

//Vue.use(SimplestPlugin)
Vue.use(OptionsPlugin)
```

```
Vue.config.productionTip = false

new Vue({
  render: h => h(App)
}).$mount('#app')
```

Now, back in `OptionsPlugin/index.js`, we will add the following code:

```
export default {
  install(Vue) {
    Vue.directive('text-length', {
      bind(el, binding, vnode) {
        const textLength = el.innerText.length;
        console.log("This element, " + el.nodeName + ", has text with "
+ textLength + " characters");
        el.style.cssText = "border: 2px solid tomato";
      }
    })
  }
}
```

Notice that we have completely omitted the `options` object in the `install` method. The reason is simple: the `options` object is optional, and not providing it will not break our code.

In the previous plugin definition, we are getting the length of the `el.innerText` string, and then we are logging it out to the console. Additionally, the `el` that has our plugin's custom `v-text-length` directive applied will also be made more noticeable with a red border.

Next, let's use the functionality from our plugin in a component's template. Specifically, we'll use it at the beginning of the `HelloWorld.vue` file inside the `src/components` folder:

```
<template>
  <div class="hello">
    <h1 v-text-length>{{ msg }}</h1>
```

Running our app in the browser at this point will produce the following message in the console:

```
This element, H1, has text with 26 characters
```

Now, we can introduce our `options` object. The purpose of the `options` object will be to allow us to customize the way in which the HTML element that is affected by the `v-text-length` directive is displayed. In other words, we can decide to give the users of our plugin the option to choose between different kinds of styles based on options that we pass in.

So, let's update our plugin with the following code:

```
const OptionsPlugin = {
  install(Vue, options) {
    Vue.directive('text-length', {
        bind(el, binding, vnode) {
            const textLength = el.innerText.length;
            console.log("This element, " + el.nodeName + ", has text with "
+ textLength + " characters");
        if (textLength < 40) {
          el.style.cssText += "border:" + options.selectedOption.plum;
        } else if (textLength >= 40) {
          el.style.cssText += "border:" + options.selectedOption.orange;
        }
        }
    })
  }
};

export default OptionsPlugin;
```

There are a few things happening in the previous code. First, we are creating an object on the fly and we are assigning it to `const OptionsPlugin`. At the bottom of the file, we are exporting the `OptionsPlugin` we have just defined.

Inside the `optionsPlugin` object, we are using a couple of if statements to serve different styles based on the length of text found in the text node of the `el` element. If the length of text is less than 40 characters, then we will assign the value `options.selectedOption.plum` to the `border` CSS property.

Otherwise, if the length of text is equal to or greater than 40 characters, we will assign the value of `options.selectedOption.orange` to the `border` CSS property inside the inline `style` attribute of the element in question.

Next, let's set these option values. We'll do that in our `main.js` file. We'll update the section where we use the plugin to the following code:

```
Vue.use(OptionsPlugin, {
  selectedOption: {
    plum: "5px dashed purple",
    orange: "10px double orange"
  }
})
```

Finally, in the `HelloWorld.vue` file, we made only a slight update. We add the plugin-defined directive to the `p` tag that follows right after the `h1` tag:

```
<template>
  <div class="hello">
    <h1 v-text-length>{{ msg }}</h1>
    <p v-text-length>
```

Now, when we run our app, we'll get the following text logged to the console:

```
This element, H1, has text with 26 characters
This element, P, has text with 121 characters
```

In our viewport, this plugin will add a dashed purple border around the `h1` tag and a double orange border around the `p` tag.

Now that we understand the basic way in which plugins can be created and used, we can think of creative ways to make our plugin do something more useful. For example, we could improve the existing plugin by adding a tooltip that would display the number of words that are present in different elements on the page. We could also add color intensity: the more words there are, the more color we could give to this "character count" badge.

Alternatively, we could list the values present in the style attribute, or the class attribute, or both. This plugin would be useful for the quick inspection of styles without opening the dev tools, which could prove useful on smaller screens or workstations that have only one screen available.

Next, we'll discuss how we can publish a Vue plugin. Specifically, we will publish the OptionsPlugin we just made.

Publishing a Vue plugin

A prerequisite to authoring an npm plugin is registering on the website and verifying your email address. Hence, the first step in authoring your Vue plugin on npm is to visit https://www.npmjs.com and register an account.

We will publish our Vue plugin on npm. First, let's check whether we already have a user. Run the following command in your console:

```
npm whoami
```

If that throws an error, you will need to create a new user by running this command:

```
npm adduser
```

Then, just follow the instructions to add yourself as the user.

Adding a simple plugin

To add a simple, one-file plugin, simply run npm init in the folder of your choice. This command will help you create a package.json file.

This is the list of questions and answers provided:

```
package name: "vue-options-plugin"
version: (1.0.0)
description: A simple Vue plugin that shows how to use the options object
entry point: "OptionsPlugin.vue"
test command:
git repository:
keywords:
license: (ISC)
About to write to ...
Is this ok? (yes)
```

The default answers that the npm init utility provides are listed in round brackets. To accept the defaults, simply press the *Enter* key. Otherwise, simply type the desired answer.

There is also the concept of scope for npm authors. Scope is simply your username. The best approach to not having to worry about scope is to have it set in your .npmrc file, via the command line, by running the following command:

```
npm init --scope=username
```

Of course, you need to replace the word username with your actual username.

Once done, run the dir command to list the contents of the folder. It should list only one file: package.json. Now, we can create another file, named OptionsPlugin.vue:

```
touch OptionsPlugin.vue
```

Let's quickly verify that our package.json file looks like this:

```
{
  "name": "vue-options-plugin",
  "version": "1.0.0",
  "description": "A simple Vue plugin that shows how to use options
object",
  "main": "OptionsPlugin.vue",
  "scripts": {
    "test": "echo \"Error: no test specified\" && exit 1"
  },
  "author": "<your-username-here>",
  "license": "ISC"
}
```

Next, let's update the OptionsPlugin.vue file with this code:

```
const OptionsPlugin = {
  install(Vue, options) {
    Vue.directive('text-length', {
        bind(el, binding, vnode) {
            const textLength = el.innerText.length;
            console.log("This element, " + el.nodeName + ", has text with "
+ textLength + " characters");
        if (textLength < 40) {
          el.style.cssText += "border:" + options.selectedOption.plum;
        } else if (textLength >= 40) {
          el.style.cssText += "border:" + options.selectedOption.orange;
        }
        }
    })
  }
};

export default OptionsPlugin;
```

Finally, let's add a README.md file. The md file extension stands for Markdown, which is a format that makes it very easy to author content online. We will add the following contents to the README:

```
# optionsplugin
<p> A demo of making a simple Vue 2 plugin and using it with values stored
in the options object. This plugin logs out to the console the number of
characters in an element. It also adds different CSS styles based on the
length of characters in the element.</p>

## Installation
```bash
 npm install --save optionsplugin
```
Configuration
```javascript
import Vue from 'vue';
import OptionsPlugin from 'optionsplugin'
Vue.use(OptionsPlugin, {
  selectedOption: {
    plum: "5px dashed purple",
    orange: "10px double orange"
  }
})
```
Usage
<p>To use it, simply add the plugin's custom directive of v-text-length to
an element in your template's code.</p>
```

This should be a good starting point for our plugin's description. We can always improve the README later. Now that we have package.json, README.md, and OptionsPlugin.vue ready, we can publish our plugin simply by running this:

```
npm publish --access=public
```

We need to provide the --access=public flag to our npm publish command, because scope packages default to private access and we need to explicitly override this setting.

Once published, our console will log out the following information:

```
+ vue-options-plugin@1.0.0
```

This is the sign that we have successfully published our plugin. Our new plugin now has its very own home, at the following URL:

`https://www.npmjs.com/package/vue-options-plugin`.

Finally, let's look how to install our newly added plugin to another project.

Installing our NPM plugin in a Vue project using Vue CLI 3

To install our Vue plugin from `npm`, we need to first create a new project. Let's run these commands:

```
vue create just-another-project
cd just-another-project
npm run-serve
```

Now, we can add our `npm` plugin by running this:

```
npm install --save vue-options-plugin
```

That's all there is to it; now, our plugin is available in our project and we can use it as described earlier, by importing it like this:

```
import VueOptionsPlugin from 'vue-options-plugin'
```

And now, we can use our plugin's functionality as needed.

Additional plugins to learn from

It is always good to look at well-coded examples of other people's code, so that we can learn from them. Some useful plugins that we can learn from and possibly contribute to are these:

- A guided tour plugin, vue-tour: `https://github.com/pulsardev/vue-tour`
- Multi-select plugin, vue-multiselect: `https://vue-multiselect.js.org/`
- A tooltip plugin, v-tooltip: `https://akryum.github.io/v-tooltip`

Summary

In this chapter, we looked at creating custom directives and custom plugins in Vue. We covered how to structure custom directives, and how to make global and local custom directives. We also looked at passing values to custom directives and working with Vue plugins. We looked at how to create a couple of custom Vue plugins. Finally, we have seen how to publish our plugin to npm and how to install it in our projects from NPM.

In the chapter that follows, we will examine how to make our apps feel more interactive with the help of transitions and animations.

Transitions and Animations

6

In this chapter, we'll look at how to use transitions and animations in Vue. This is a large topic that would take a lot more than a chapter to cover. Hence, we will deal with some fundamental concepts that we can build upon in the future.

We will focus on the following topics:

- Understanding CSS transitions and animations
- Implementing transitions with the `transition` component
- Working with CSS transitions and animations in Vue
- Integrating with third-party CSS and JS libraries
- Binding CSS styles
- Working with transition groups
- JavaScript animation hooks

After reading this chapter, you should have a solid understanding of how transitions and animations are used in Vue.

Transitions and animations in CSS

To understand how Vue.js deals with transitions and animations, we will first need to have a quick refresher on how they work in CSS. We will focus on the bare basics, with the goal of revisiting the principles that govern transitions and animations. We will also look at their differences. The goal is to be able to understand better how Vue helps, rather than dive deep into the nuances of transitions and animations.

How CSS transitions work

When we hover over an element, we put that element in a hover state. When the user triggers a hover state through their interaction with our web page, we might want to *emphasize* that this change of state has occurred.

To emphasize that change of state, we could, for example, change the CSS `background-color` property on that element when the user hovers over it.

This is where CSS transitions come in. When we write code for CSS transitions, we *instruct* the browser on how it will display changes made to that specific CSS property—in our example, the `background-color` property.

Let's say we have an HTML `button` element. This element has its CSS property of `background-color` set to `red`:

```
button {
  background-color: red;
}
```

When a user hovers over the button, we want to change the value of the `background-color` property from `red` to `blue`. We'll do that like this:

```
button:hover {
  background-color: blue;
}
```

The sample code is available here: `https://codepen.io/AjdinImsirovic/pen/LJKJYY`.

However, this change of color is sudden. To *smoothly transition* a CSS property of an HTML element from one value to the other, we use the CSS `transition` property. The `transition` property is a shorthand CSS property. It is just another CSS property we specify on the targeted element—the one to which we want to apply this smooth transition.

In our case, we want to smoothly transition our button from the red background to the blue background. We will simply add the shorthand `transition` property on the button element, and set two values on this `transition` property:

```
button {
 background-color: red;
 transition: background-color 4s;
}
button:hover {
 background-color: blue;
}
```

This is the formula:

```
transition: property-to-transition transition-duration, property-to-
transition transition-duration
```

In our example, we're specifying the duration for only one property, but we can add more, as needed. The previous example can be found at `https://codepen.io/AjdinImsirovic/pen/rqBqYN`.

How CSS animations work

In the previous example, we saw a simple transition. In this example, we will convert the transition into an animation. The updated CSS code will look like this:

```
button {
  background-color: red;
}
button:hover {
  animation: change-color 4s;
}
@keyframes change-color {
  0% {
    background: red;
  }
  100% {
    background: blue;
  }
}
```

In the previous code, we have converted our simple CSS transition into a CSS animation.

This example can be found at this link: `https://codepen.io/AjdinImsirovic/pen/WaNePm`.

However, it does not work 100% the same. When we hover over the button, we don't get the exact same behavior we had in the transition example. The reason is that we have specified the initial state (as `0%`) and the final state (as `100%`) of our animation. So, we are effectively mapping over the behavior we had in the transition example, to behavior in the animation example.

However, when we remove the mouse pointer from the button, the animation does not rewind to the initial state, but rather abruptly cuts back to the original background color of red. In CSS, there is no `mouseout` property.

We could, however, add additional steps in between. For example, we could set the background color to green at 50% of our change animation. The result can be seen at this URL: `https://codepen.io/AjdinImsirovic/pen/QZWWje`.

Before we dive into how Vue implements transitions and animations, let's look at the differences between them in CSS.

Differences between transitions and animations in CSS

Here are two quick, incomplete lists of the differences between transitions and animations in CSS.

Rules for CSS transitions

Here are some important rules of CSS transitions:

- Transitions only have implied start and end states
- The way that a transition will be performed is decided by the browser; in other words, the browser decides how it will perform the in-between steps of the transition
- We can only point the browser to the exact CSS property we want transitioned, and the duration, easing, and so on
- Transitions are *triggered; t*he trigger can be a hover or an element appearing on the page (via JavaScript)
- Transitions can't be looped
- Transitions are played in reverse when the trigger state (the hover state) is reverted, that is, when the mouse is *unhovered*
- Transition syntax is simpler than the syntax for animations

Next, let's list the important concepts of CSS animations.

Rules for CSS animations

What follows is an incomplete list of rules for CSS animations:

- Animations allow us to specify initial state, in-between state(s), and end state of our CSS properties

- There can be as many steps as we need in our CSS animations
- We can delay animations, play them *x* number of times (to infinity), or play them in the opposite direction
- Animations don't have to be triggered, but they can be

With these basic distinctions out of the way, let's next look at how to deal with transitions and animations in Vue.

The transition element in Vue

Let's look at the previous example of CSS-only transitions, ported into Vue. In the following example, the first button is wrapped inside a custom component, while the second button is just the regular HTML button element. They still both share the same styles, as specified in the app's CSS:

```
<!-- HTML -->
<div id="app">
  <button>Hover me!</button>
  <custom-component></custom-component>
</div>

// JS
Vue.component('customComponent', {
  template: `
    <button>Hover me too!</button>
  `
});
new Vue({
  el: '#app'
});

/* CSS */
button {
  background-color: red;
  transition: background-color 4s;
}
button:hover {
  background-color: blue;
}
/* some additional styling */
* {
  border: none;
  color: white;
  padding: 10px;
```

```
      font-size: 18px;
      font-weight: 600;
  }
```

The previous code can be found here: `https://codepen.io/AjdinImsirovic/pen/`
`vVYERO`. As can be seen in the example, in this case, Vue does not diverge from the way that
transitions and animations work in plain HTML and CSS.

Vue is not designed to override the normal use case for CSS transitions and animations, but
rather to work alongside them with one specific goal: to transition the appearance and
removal of its *components* on the screen. This addition and removal of components is done
with the help of Vue's `transition` element.

For example, when you want to have an event in one component to affect the addition and
removal of another component, you simply wrap that other component in a `transition`
element. To build from the previous examples with plain CSS, here is a simple
implementation in Vue:

```
<!-- HTML -->
<div id="app">
  <button v-on:click="show = !show">
    Show? {{ show }}
  </button>
  <transition>
    <span v-if="show">
      <custom-component></custom-component>
    </span>
  </transition>
</div>

// JS
Vue.component('customComponent', {
  template: `
    <button>Hover me!</button>
  `
});
new Vue({
  el: '#app',
  data: {
    show: true
  }
});

/* CSS is the same as in the previous example */
```

The example code is available here: `https://codepen.io/AjdinImsirovic/pen/ZqExJO`.

 If you need the element to appear smoothly on the initial page load, without conditions, then you can use the `appear` attribute on your transition wrapper, like this: `<transition appear>`.

What is happening in the previous code is that we are conditionally toggling the mounting of the `custom-component` element based on whether the user has clicked the first button or not. Note that the original CSS transition is still behaving the exact same way in both buttons. When we hover over either of them, we still get the four-second transition of background color from red to blue. The browser still takes care of the *inverted* transition of a button's background when we hover away from either of the buttons.

However, the mounting of the second button on the screen comes without any transitions. The second button simply appears and disappears upon clicking the first, without any easing in or out.

To achieve this gradual appearance and removal, the `transition` element comes with built-in CSS class names. These built-in transition class names are also called **animation hooks**. These animation hooks describe the beginning state, the end state, and the in-between state for component(s) wrapped inside that `transition` element; that is, they describe in what way the affected components will toggle on and off the screen.

We can add animation hooks to either *enter* transitions or to *leave* transitions. Enter transition classes are `v-enter`, `v-enter-active`, and `v-enter-to`. Leave transition classes are `v-leave`, `v-leave-active`, and `v-leave-to`.

Setting up the enter transition

To build on the previous example, we will employ these animation hooks to make the second button's appearance and disappearance smoother. The only difference between the previous example and this one is the addition of animation hooks in our CSS:

```
.v-enter {
  opacity: 0;
}
.v-enter-active {
 transition: opacity 3s;
}
```

The code for this example can be found at the following link: `https://codepen.io/AjdinImsirovic/pen/MPWVNm`.

If we imagine the appearance of the second button as a regular CSS transition, then the `.v-enter` animation hook would be the initial transition state, `.v-enter-active` would be the in-between steps, and `.v-enter-to` would be the final transition state, that is, what the element will transition *to*.

Because we have not used the `.v-enter-to` animation hook in our example, the behavior we get is as follows: when the first button is clicked, the second button takes three seconds to change (transition) its opacity from the initial value of zero to the implied value of one. This takes care of our enter transition.

Setting up the leave transition

There is a slight issue with our previous example: when we click the first button again, the second button will disappear instantly, because its opacity value will be reset to zero without any transition. The reason for this is simple: we have not specified any *leave* transition hooks, so the button just disappears. We'll fix that in the next example, by simply specifying the leave transitions, like this:

```
.v-leave {
  opacity: 1;
}
.v-leave-active {
  transition: opacity 3s;
}
.v-leave-to {
  opacity: 0;
}
```

The full code can be found here: `https://codepen.io/AjdinImsirovic/pen/XxWqOy`. What we are doing in this code is this: when the component needs to be animated out, our transition's initial state is `.v-leave`. The CSS declaration in the `.v-leave` animation hook is `opacity: 1`. Next, we specify the in-between steps: the CSS property to be transitioned, namely `opacity`, and the duration of the transition: `3s`. Finally, we specify the finished state for our transition, where `opacity` gets set to the value of zero.

What we can conclude from these examples is that the *leave* transitions' animation hooks (`v-leave`, `v-leave-active`, and `v-leave-to`) should be *a mirror image*—figuratively speaking—in comparison to the enter transitions' animation hooks (`v-enter`, `v-enter-active`, and `v-enter-to`).

We can also conclude that the transition component and the animation hooks that come along with it are to be used for mounting and unmounting the components on the screen. When transitioning a component on and off the screen, the animation hooks' natural progression is this:

```
.v-enter --> .v-enter-active --> .v-enter-to --> .v-leave --> v-leave-
active --> .v-leave-to
```

We can also group certain CSS selectors that share the same values, as follows:

```
.v-enter, .v-leave-to {
  opacity: 0;
}
.v-enter-active, .v-leave-active {
  transition: opacity 3s;
}
.v-enter-to, .v-leave {
  opacity: 1;
}
```

This example can be found at the following web address: `https://codepen.io/AjdinImsirovic/pen/dgyKMG`.

As can be seen here, `.v-enter` (the initial enter animation hook) gets combined with `.v-leave-to` (the last leave animation hook) precisely because the transition must be played in reverse to get the most expected behavior. Similarly, we are grouping the in-between steps, the `-active` hooks, to have the same `transition` CSS property. Finally, the enter animation's final hook needs to share the CSS declaration with the initial leave animation hook. Also, since the `.v-enter-to` and the `.v-leave` values are implied by default, we can even omit them and still have a working component transition, similar to the one described in the official documentation: `https://vuejs.org/v2/guide/transitions.html#Transitioning-Single-Elements-Components`.

To make things simpler to reason about, in our most recent example we have also changed the `data` option's `show` key to the value of `false`. That way, initially the component is not mounted to the DOM. Only when the user clicks on the first button will the second button's enter animation hooks kick in and smoothly transition the component in. On another click, the second button's leave animation hook will kick in and transition the component out in reverse. This is important, since initially we had the enter animation transition the unmounting of the component and the leave animation transition the mounting of it back into the page, which possibly makes things slightly more difficult to reason about.

Naming transition components

We can give our transition elements the `name` attribute. Doing this changes the naming convention for animation hooks. For example, if we give our transition the name of `named`, then the animation hooks will need to be renamed as follows. For every transition class, we'll replace the beginning `v-` with the value of the `name` attribute. Hence, `v-enter` will become `named-enter`, `v-leave` will become `named-leave`, and so on.

Let's rewrite the previous example with a named transition:

```html
<!-- HTML -->
<div id="app">
  <button v-on:click="show = !show">
    Show? {{ show }}
  </button>
  <transition name="named">
    <span v-if="show">
      <custom-component></custom-component>
    </span>
  </transition>
</div>
```

```css
/* CSS */
/* 'named' transition */
.named-enter, .named-leave-to {
  opacity: 0;
}
.named-enter-active, .named-leave-active {
  transition: opacity 3s;
}
.named-enter-to, .named-leave {
  opacity: 1;
}
```

```js
// JS is unchanged
```

The code for this example is available in this CodePen: `https://codepen.io/AjdinImsirovic/pen/MPWqgm`.

CSS animations with transition component

CSS animations are also employed with the help of the transition component. Here is an example of the previous example with CSS transition, converted into using a CSS animation. We'll begin with HTML:

```
<div id="app">
  <button v-on:click="show = !show">
    Show? {{ show }}
  </button>
  <transition name="converted">
    <span v-if="show">
      <custom-component></custom-component>
    </span>
  </transition>
</div>
```

Next, we'll add the following JavaScript code:

```
Vue.component('customComponent', {
  template: `
    <button>Lorem ipsum</button>
  `
});
new Vue({
  el: '#app',
  data: {
    show: false
  }
});
```

We'll add a few simple styles too:

```
/* 'named' transition is replaced with 'converted' animation */
.converted-enter-active {
  animation: converted .5s;
}
.converted-leave-active {
  animation: converted .5s reverse;
}
@keyframes converted {
  0% { opacity: 0; }
  35% { background-color: purple; }
  65% { background-color: green; }
  100% { opacity: 1; }
}
/* other styles */
button {
```

```
    background-color: red;
    transition: background-color 4s;
  }
button:hover {
    background-color: blue;
  }
/* some additional styling */
* {
    border: none;
    color: white;
    padding: 10px;
    font-size: 18px;
    font-weight: 600;
  }
span {
    display: inline-block;
  }
```

The code for this example is available here: `https://codepen.io/AjdinImsirovic/pen/vVEXEv`. The converted animation is exactly the same as the previous example with CSS transitions, save for the change in animation behavior at 35% and 65% of animation completion. The effect that we get is sort of like a border color effect, even though we are changing the `background-color` property of this element. This confirms a few conclusions we already discussed, namely the following:

- The `transition` element in Vue affects the appearance and disappearance of the entire `<transition>` component, rather than its contents
- The actual animation can have as many steps as needed; in other words, to get the exact same effect as we had in the CSS transition example, it would be enough to simply remove the steps we specified at 35% and 65% of animation completion

In the next section, we'll discuss custom transition classes.

Custom transition classes

Custom transition classes are great when we want to add functionality from a third-party CSS animation library. In this example, we'll be using the `Animate.CSS` animation library, available here: `https://daneden.github.io/animate.css/`.

The official documentation covers the use of custom transition classes sufficiently at this URL: `https://vuejs.org/v2/guide/transitions.html#Custom-Transition-Classes`.

The only thing to add is the example we have been building on, available here: `https://codepen.io/AjdinImsirovic/pen/rqazXZ`.

The code for the example is as follows. First, we'll start with the HTML:

```
<div id="app">
  <button v-on:click="show = !show">
    Show? {{ show }}
  </button>
  <transition :duration="4000"
      name="converted"
      enter-active-class="rubberBand animated"
      leave-active-class="bounceOut animated">
        <div v-if="show">
          <custom-component>
          </custom-component>
        </div>
  </transition>
</div>
```

Next, let's see the JavaScript:

```
Vue.component('customComponent', {
  template: `
    <button>Lorem ipsum</button>
  `
});
new Vue({
  el: '#app',
  data: {
    show: false
  }
});
```

Finally, inside our styles, we'll set up some basic CSS declarations:

```
button {
  background-color: red;
  transition: background-color 4s;
}
button:hover {
  background-color: blue;
}

* {
```

```
    border: none;
    color: white;
    padding: 10px;
    font-size: 18px;
    font-weight: 600;
  }
* { overflow: hidden }
```

Basically, we specify attributes that have the same names as animation hooks, plus the additional -class at the end of the attribute name. Hence, the default v-enter-active CSS class becomes the custom enter-active-class HTML attribute. We then give this custom HTML attribute a value we choose. The value we give it is the class name of the effect we want to use from our CSS animation library we previously picked—in this case, the Animate.CSS library. In the previous code, we have also set the :duration prop, specifying the duration of the transition to be exactly 4000 miliseconds. Practically, in our example, this will only have an effect if the :duration prop we set is shorter than the duration of animations we provided from the third-party library. For example, try setting the :duration prop to 100 milliseconds and see the animation chopped off. This can create some interesting effects.

Combining transition modes, duration, keys, and v-if

Transition modes are used when we want to smoothly remove one element from the screen and seamlessly replace it with another one. The default transition mode that the <transition> component comes with, without any tweaks needed, is the simultaneous transition: one element is removed at the same time that another is added.

However, there are some transitions is which it would be better to have the new element appear, and only when this transition is complete does the old element get removed. This transition mode is referred to as the in-out transition mode. To add it, we simply use the custom mode HTML attribute, and give it the value of in-out, like this:

```
<transition mode="in-out">
```

Alternatively, we might want to use the out-in transition mode, where we first have the old element transition out, and only then, when the transition is complete, the new element transitions in.

Let's see this in practice. The example is available at this pen: https://codepen.io/AjdinImsirovic/pen/yRyPed.

Here is the HTML:

```html
<div id="app">
  <transition name="smooth" mode="out-in" :duration="500">
      <button v-if="show"
              key="first"
              v-on:click="show = !show">
                Show? {{ show }}
      </button>
      <button v-else
              key="second"
              v-on:click="show = !show">
                Show? {{ show }}
      </button>
  </transition>
  <transition :duration="1000"
      enter-active-class="slideInDown animated"
      leave-active-class="slideOutDown animated">
        <div v-if="show">
          <custom-component>
          </custom-component>
        </div>
  </transition>
</div>
```

We are still using the same JS:

```js
Vue.component('customComponent', {
  template: `
    <button>Lorem ipsum</button>
  `
});
new Vue({
  el: '#app',
  data: {
    show: false
  }
});
```

There are some changes in our CSS:

```css
/* CSS classes used are imported from the Animate CSS library
and can be found in Settings of this pen */
/* other styles */
.smooth-enter, .smooth-leave-to {
  opacity: 0;
}
.smooth-enter-active, .smooth-leave-active {
```

```
    transition: opacity .5s;
}
.smooth-enter-to, .smooth-leave {
  opacity: 1;
}

button {
  background-color: red;
  transition: background-color 4s;
}
button:hover {
  background-color: blue;
}

* {
  border: none;
  color: white;
  padding: 10px;
  font-size: 18px;
  font-weight: 600;
}
* { overflow: hidden }
```

We are switching on and off between two `button` elements inside our transition. Since these two have the same tag name, we need to give them different `key` attributes so Vue can distinguish them.

Also, we are rendering our buttons conditionally. While we are keeping the check of `v-if="show"` in the first button, in the second button we are simply using the `v-else` directive, without giving it a value to check against.

Binding CSS styles in Vue

In this section, we'll discuss how to animate other parts of the page when a component is mounted or removed. For that, we will use the `v-bind` directive, and as we have seen in the previous chapters, we can use this directive to bind to HTML attributes. Once bound, these attributes can then be manipulated from our Vue instance.

The example for which we will demonstrate CSS style binding is a simple onboarding demo. Onboarding, in terms of web page usability, is the practice of showing new users of a web app the overall functionality that a web page has, which is achieved by highlighting a certain section of a page and showing a popover with some information that further describes the functionality at that specific step of the onboarding process.

To begin with, we need to understand that we can statically bind CSS classes by passing the value of the `v-bind:class` directive as an object, as in the following example:

```
<p v-bind:class="{}">Some text...</p>
```

Inside the object, we can simply add CSS classes as keys, and Boolean `true` and `false` as values. CSS values that are set to `true` will be used, otherwise, they won't, as in the following example:

```
<button v-bind:class="{'btn': true, 'btn-lg': true, 'btn-primary': true,
'btn-secondary': false}">A button</button>
```

In this example, we are using the Bootstrap framework's CSS classes. We are setting the button to the class of `btn-primary`, as it is set to `true`, rather than the `btn-secondary`, which is set to false.

Because the `v-bind` directive allows us to programatically control HTML attributes, we might make our app switch CSS classes on a click. For example, in a basic Vue app, we might do this in our HTML:

```
<button v-bind:class="'btn':true','btn-lg':true, 'btn-primary':true, 'btn-
secondary':btnClicked">
A button
</button>
```

In the previous code, we are setting the classes of `btn`, `btn-lg`, and `btn-primary` to `true`, and we are setting the value of `btn-secondary` to `btnClicked`. Next, we're going to set the value of `btnClicked` to `false` in our JavaScript:

```
data: {
  btnClicked: false,
}
```

Finally, we'll add the click event to our button, so when it's clicked, the value of `btnClicked` will be toggled from `true` to `false`, and vice versa. Here is the code:

```
<button
  v-on:click="btnClicked = !btnClicked"
  v-bind:class="'btn':true','btn-lg':true, 'btn-primary':true, 'btn-
secondary':btnClicked">
    A button
</button>
```

This example is available at this URL: `https://codepen.io/AjdinImsirovic/pen/KGVvML`.

We can further expand on this example by using the `data` property to store groups of CSS classes, and a JavaScript ternary expression to check whether the `btnClicked` value is currently set to `true` or `false`:

```html
<!-- HTML -->
<div id="app" class="p-4">
  <h1>Improving dynamic CSS classes example</h1>
  <p class="lead">Click the button below a few times</p>
  <button
    v-on:click="btnClicked = !btnClicked"
    v-bind:class="btnClicked ? btnPrimary : btnSecondary">
      btnClicked {{ btnClicked }}
  </button>
</div>
```

```js
// JS
new Vue({
  el: '#app',
  data() {
    return {
      btnClicked: false,
      btnPrimary: 'btn btn-lg btn-primary',
      btnSecondary: 'btn btn-lg btn-secondary'
    }
  }
})
```

The code for the previous example is available at `https://codepen.io/AjdinImsirovic/pen/wYMEJQ`.

Animating a button on click with dynamic CSS classes

Now, we are ready to add animations by virtue of simply adding additional CSS classes from the aforementioned Animate.CSS animation library. The updates to the previous example's code are minimal. We are only adding two CSS classes here:

```
btnPrimary: 'btn btn-lg btn-primary bounce animated',
```

Of course, we also had to include the Animate.CSS library, as can be seen here: `https://codepen.io/AjdinImsirovic/pen/RerEyy`. To add the animation on both clicks, we simply alter the entry for `btnSecondary` to this:

```
btnSecondary: 'btn btn-lg btn-secondary tada animated'
```

Now, the button will be animated on every click.

Working with transition groups

While a single transition component is used to wrap around a single element, transition groups are used for animating multiple elements. They come with an additional animation hook: `v-move`.

In the example that follows, we'll build simple functionality where users can award a piece of content online with an **applause**, a concept similar to the **clap** feature of `https://medium.com/`, which works as follows: if a visitor to the website likes a piece of content, they can award it with *claps*, by clicking the **clap** button up to 50 times. hence, the claps feature works like a kind of a counter of how much a piece of content is appreciated by the website visitors.

In our implementation, we will combine the features we have already covered. The difference is, instead of a transition, we will use the `transition-group` component. This is the HTML code:

```html
<!-- HTML -->
<div id="app">
    <div class="tale">
        <transition-group>
          <button
                class="bare"
                key="howManyClaps"
                v-if="clapCount">
                    {{ clapCount }}
          </button>
          <button
                class="fa fa-thumbs-o-up animated orange"
                key="theClapButton"
                v-on:click="aClap()">
          </button>
        </transition-group>
    </div>
</div>
```

Here is the JS code:

```
new Vue({
  el: "#app",
  data: {
    clapCount: false
  },
  methods: {
    aClap() {
      var target = document.querySelector('.fa-thumbs-o-up');
      if (!target.classList.contains('wobble')) {
        target.classList.add('wobble');
      }
      setTimeout(function() {
        target.classList.remove('wobble')}, 300
      )
      if (this.clapCount < 10) {
        this.clapCount++
      } else {
        target.classList.remove('orange','wobble')
      }
    }
  }
});
```

And here is the CSS code:

```
button.bare {
  font-size: 30px;
  background: white;
  border: none;
  margin: 0 20px;
}
button:focus.bare, button:focus.fa {
  outline: 0;
}
button.fa {
  cursor: pointer;
  color: white;
  padding: 20px;
  border-radius: 50%;
  font-size: 30px;
  border: none;
}
.orange {
  background: orange;
}
```

```
/* animation hooks */
.v-enter,
.v-leave-to{
  opacity: 0;
  transform: translate(1000px, 500px);
}
.v-enter-active,
.v-leave-active {
  transition: opacity 5s, transform 1s
}
```

The previous code is available as a pen at this URL: `https://codepen.io/AjdinImsirovic/pen/JmXJgd`.

There are several things happening in this code. In HTML, we are using the `transition-group` component to work with two buttons. In JS, we set up the logic for the behavior of our claps. We begin the `clapCount` set to `false`, which coerces to zero. In CSS, we style the buttons and we employ the animation hooks. The `transform` and `transition` values have been set to extreme values, to be able to understand better how they work by playing around with the values (for instance, `1000 px` for the translate on the X axis, and `500 px` for the translate on the Y axis).

JavaScript animation hooks

We can use Vue's `transition` classes as JavaScript methods. Just like lifecycle hooks, we don't have to access any of them. Or we can cherry-pick those that we want to use. To begin, inside our Vue constructor's `methods` option, we could specify what to do with all of them:

```
methods: {
  // ENTER transitions...
  beforeEnter: function(el) {},
  enter: function(el, done) {},
  afterEnter: function(el) {},
  enterCancelled: function(el) {},
  // LEAVE transitions...
  beforeLeave: function(el) {},
  leave: function(el,done) {},
  afterLeave: function(el) {},
  leaveCancelled: function(el) {},
}
```

As we can see, we have four methods for enter transitions and another four methods for leave transitions. All of the methods take in the `el` argument and the `enter` and `leave` methods also take in the `done` argument to signify the completion of an animation. If the `done` argument was not used, the hooks would be called without waiting for the `done` callback to complete, and the transition would be completed at once.

Let's rewrite the previous example using these JavaScript animation hooks. To keep things easy to understand, we will integrate the official documentation's example into our example, so that we can see how this example works when the animation hooks are called via JavaScript only.

This is the code we will use in our HTML:

```
<transition
  v-on:before-enter="beforeEnter"
  v-on:enter="enter"
  v-on:leave="leave"
  v-bind:css="false">
<p v-if="show" style="font-size:25px">Animation example with velocity</p>
</transition>
```

This is the code we will use in our JS:

```
new Vue({
  el: "#app",
  data: {
    clapCount: false
  },
  methods: {
    beforeEnter: function(el) {
      el.style.opacity = 0
    },
      enter: function (el, done) {
      Velocity(el, { opacity: 1, fontSize: '1.4em' }, { duration: 300 })
      Velocity(el, { fontSize: '1em' }, { complete: done })
    },
    leave: function (el, done) {
      Velocity(el, { translateX: '15px', rotateZ: '50deg' }, {
      duration: 600 })
      Velocity(el, { rotateZ: '100deg' }, { loop: 2 })
      Velocity(el, {
        rotateZ: '45deg',
        translateY: '30px',
        translateX: '30px',
        opacity: 0
      }, { complete: done })},
    aClap() {
```

```
      var target = document.querySelector('.fa-thumbs-o-up');
      if (!target.classList.contains('wobble')) {
        target.classList.add('wobble');
      }
      setTimeout(function() {
        target.classList.remove('wobble')}, 300
      )
      if (this.clapCount < 10) {
        this.clapCount++
      } else {
        target.classList.remove('orange','wobble')
      }
    }
  }
});
```

Here is the CSS:

```
button.bare {
  font-size: 30px;
  background: white;
  border: none;
  margin: 0 20px;
}
button:focus.bare, button:focus.fa {
  outline: 0;
}
button.fa {
  cursor: pointer;
  color: white;
  padding: 20px;
  border-radius: 50%;
  font-size: 30px;
  border: none;
}
.orange {
  background: orange;
}
```

The example is available here: `https://codepen.io/AjdinImsirovic/pen/PyzqxM`.

With this understanding, it is easy to change parameters in the specific methods inside our Vue constructor to achieve the desired effect for our JavaScript-powered animations.

Summary

In this chapter, we looked at working with transitions and animations in Vue.js. Specifically, we examined how transitions and animations work in CSS. We examined the differences between transitions and animations in CSS and established the rules for both. We worked with the transition and transition-group elements in Vue, and we discussed animation hooks and their grouping into enter and leave transitions. We saw how transition components can be named and, given key values and how we can assign custom transition classes for easier integration with third-party animation libraries.

We explained when to use transition modes and how to further tweak our animations with `:duration` and `conditional` directives. We mentioned the importance of binding CSS styles in Vue and how this approach can be used for adding animations to our web apps. Finally, we saw how to convert CSS class-based transitions into JavaScript-based animation hooks.

In the next chapter, we will discuss how to use Vuex.

7
Using Vuex

In this chapter, we'll learn how to manage complex state in Vue by using Vuex. Vuex helps deal with the issue of managing state and deeply nested components in Vue apps.

At the end of this chapter, you will understand what problems Vuex solves and how it solves them, and you should understand where all the moving parts fit in. You will also know how to build a simple Vuex app and the approach to take when thinking about extending it.

Specifically, we will go over these topics:

- Understanding state
- State management, data stores, and one-way data flows
- Hot reloading
- Building a very simple Vuex app
- How to update state from Vue DevTools' Vuex tab
- Building a more complex Vuex app

Let's begin by understanding exactly what state is.

What is state?

An application's state is all its data at a point in time. Since we are usually concerned with the current app's state, we could rephrase this to the following: the state is an app's data as it is right now, resulting from the previous steps that our app took and based on functions inside the app responding to the user interacting with it.

So, what is it in our app that changes its state? Functions, of course. The user interacts with our app, which triggers functions to change the current state to some other state.

However, as our apps grow, it is not uncommon to have components nesting several levels deep. If we say that state is the **source of truth** for how our app should display on the screen at any given time, then it would be beneficial to us to make that source of truth as easy to reason about and as simple to work with as possible.

Unfortunately, in complex apps, this is not so easy. Any part of our app, any component inside our app might affect any other part of our app. Managing state in our apps becomes a bit like playing a game of whack-a-mole: an interaction in one section of our app will result in something else *popping* out of place in some other part of our app.

Reasoning about best practice for how to manage complex state in frontend apps has led to concepts such as the **data store** and **one-way data flows**.

State management, data stores, and one-way data flows

A common solution to the problem of managing complex state is the idea of a store: a single source of truth that keeps all of the data of our app's state. Once we have that central location—**the store**—we can reason about state a lot easier, because now it is only a matter of sending the state data to those components that need to have it at any time in the app's life cycle.

To make the state updates simpler, we need to limit the ways in which these updates can be made. This is where one-way data flows come in. With one-way data flows, we specify rules on exactly how data can flow inside our app, which means that there are now only so many expected ways in which data (state) can flow through our apps, making it easier to reason about state and debug state when needed. This approach is also a great time saver, since now we as developers know what to expect; that is, to look for spots where we know state is **mutable**.

The Vuex state management pattern

Vuex is a plugin of Vue, developed by Vue's core team. The setup is quite easy. If you need a quick prototype, you can simply add the Vuex library from the settings inside CodePen online editor, as explained in `Chapter 1`, *Introducing Vue*.

You can also install it via npm, with this command:

```
npm install --save vuex
```

When trying to understand how Vuex works, you'll usually find references online that describe Vuex as a state management pattern that is heavily influenced by Flux. This is true in part, but it is interesting to note that Flux itself was inspired by the Elm architecture. Be that as it may, in Vuex, the data flows as follows:

- **Vue components** to actions
- **Actions** to mutations
- **Mutations** to state
- **State** to Vue components

The data always flows in one way, ending up where it began, with updates made to components, which then *dispatch actions*, which then *commit mutations*, which then *mutate state*, which then *renders components*, and the cycle repeats. So, looking at the one-way data flow from a slightly different angle, we could rephrase it, focusing on the verbs to describe what happens to the data in the store:

- Actions are *dispatched*
- Mutations are *committed*
- State is *mutated*
- Components are *rendered*

Looking at the one-way data flow again, we can now describe the data flow using these nouns: *components*, *actions*, *mutations*, and *state*. Describing the data flow using verbs, we can view this progression as follows: *dispatch, commit, mutate and render*.

Both of these ways of viewing the flow of data in Vuex are two sides of the same coin, the same cycle of state updates, and so thus it would not hurt to commit both of these short lists to memory, as it will help speed up the understanding of basic Vuex concepts.

To visually reinforce these explanations, a diagram of this one-way data flow is available in the official Vuex docs, at this URL: `https://vuex.vuejs.org/vuex.png`.

You might ask, why this indirect approach? Why can't components directly mutate state? There are two main reasons for this: first, since asynchronous code is simply a matter of fact in the JavaScript world, a choice was made to separate asynchronous and synchronous operations in Vuex. Hence, actions were set to be asynchronous, so they can, for example, fetch some data from the server, and only when this asynchronous data fetching is complete can they then *commit mutations*; since mutations are strictly synchronous, it wouldn't make sense to call them before the call to server has been completed. Second, this way of separating concerns enables easier tracking of state changes, which even includes time travel debugging: rerunning mutations chronologically to track changes to state and hunt down bugs.

 In the Vuex state management pattern, components can never directly mutate global state. Mutations do that.

In the next section, we'll look at each of these building blocks.

The store

The **store** needs to be added to the Vue instance root, so that all components can share this centralized, global state. Usually, we declare the store as `const`, and then later on in the code, we add it inside the object literal that we pass as the argument to the Vue constructor, like this:

```
const store = new Vuex.Store({
  // store details go here
})
new Vue({
 el: '#app',
 store: store,
 // etc
})
```

Next, we'll learn about getters.

Getters in the Vuex store

Our store can also have getters. Getters allow us to return values from the state in templates. They are a bit like computed values. They are read-only, meaning they cannot change the state. Their responsibility is only to read it and make some non-destructive manipulations of it. However, the underlying data is not mutated.

So, we use getters in the store to perform some non-destructive work on the global state. What do we then do with them? How do we use them? We use them on the other side of our app – inside a component—where we use `computed` and return the value of getters from the store.

Vuex store mutations

Mutations, as the name implies, mutate the state, and are synchronous. Functions that mutate state receive arguments: the existing state and the payload. The payload argument is optional. They are responsible for directly updating the state in Vuex. You can execute a mutation from an action with this syntax: `state.commit`.

Actions in Vuex store

Actions update the state asynchronously and indirectly, by calling one or more mutations we defined in the store. So, actions call as many mutations as needed. On the other side, inside components, to execute an action we use the store's dispatch values, using this syntax: `store.dispatch`.

Let's now extend our boilerplate code to include what we just discussed:

```
const store = new Vuex.Store({
  // store details go here; they usually have:
  state: {
    // state specified here
  },
  getters: {
    // getters are like computed values - they don't mutate state
  },
 mutations: {
   // they mutate the state and are synchronous,
   // functions that mutate state can have arguments; these arguments are
called 'payload'
  },
  actions: {
    // asynchronous functions that commit mutations
  }
})
new Vue({
 el: '#app',
 store,
 // etc
})
```

As we can see in the Vue constructor, with ES6 syntax, it is possible to simplify the `store:` `store` key-value pair inside the constructor's object literal argument and just use `store`.

Hot reloading

Another popular concept that was brought about by the rise of Webpack is hot reloading. When your app is running, upon updating a file—for example, adding some changes to scoped styles in one of your components—Webpack will hot-reload the updated file without using state in your app. In other words, it will not reload the entire page, but rather only the part of your app that was affected by the change. The reason why this is useful is because, with hot module replacement the state will be kept, which would not be possible if the page was refreshed. This comes with the added benefit of faster development time and seamless experience of updates in the browser.

Building a fruit counter app with Vuex

The app that we will build is just a simple fruit counter app. The goal is to help the user make sure to eat five pieces of fruit daily, and we will set up a simple app that will start with five pieces of fruit to eat and, each time we click the button, it will decrement the number by `1`. That way, we can keep track of our healthy eating goals.

We will begin our app by setting the initial state, with only one key-value pair in it:

```
const store = new Vuex.Store({
  state: {
    count: 5
  },
```

Next, we will set up `getters`. As we learned already, `getters` only return state:

```
  getters: {
    counter(state) {
      return state.count;
    }
  },
```

Next, we will add two mutations: the first mutation, `decrementCounter`, will operate on the counter by decrementing it by the value stored in the payload argument. We will decrement the value of state.count until it reaches `0`. To make sure the value of `state.count` cannot be less then `0`, we'll check it with the ternary statement and set its value accordingly.

The second mutation, `resetCounter`, will reset the value of the counter to the initial state:

```
mutations: {
  decrementCounter(state, payload) {
    state.count = state.count - payload;
    state.count<0 ? state.count=0 : state.count
  },
  resetCounter(state) {
    state.count = 5;
  }
},
```

Next, we are setting up two actions, `decrement` and `reset`:

```
actions: {
  decrement(state, payload) {
    state.commit("decrementCounter", payload);
  },
  reset(state) {
    state.commit("resetCounter");
  }
}
```

Finally, we're setting up our app, and specifying the `el`, `store`, `computed`, and `methods` options inside its Vue constructor:

```
const app = new Vue({
  el: "#app",
  store: store,
  computed: {
    count() {
      return store.getters.counter;
    }
  },
  methods: {
    eatFruit(amount) {
      store.dispatch("decrement", amount);
    },
    counterReset() {
      store.dispatch("reset");
    }
  }
});
```

Next, in our HTML, we set up the structure of our simple app:

```
<div id="app">
 <h1>Fruit to eat: {{count}}</h1>
 <button v-on:click="eatFruit(1)">Eat fruit!</button>
 <button v-on:click="counterReset()">Reset the counter</button>
</div>
```

The working example can be found at the following URL: `https://codepen.io/AjdinImsirovic/pen/aRmENx`.

Using the Vue DevTools plugin to track our Vuex state

If you type `vuejs devtools` into the search field of the Chrome extensions web store, you'll get a few results. The first result is the stable version of the official plugin. The second result is the Vue DevTools extension's beta version. To see all of the options that are being developed and see where this plugin is going, it's good to install the beta version. Interestingly, both versions display the same information once open in Chrome DevTools. Currently, the message reads `Ready. Detected Vue 2.5.17-beta.0`.

When compared with the regular version, the experimental version comes with a few more tabs, namely `routing` and `performance`. However, even the existing tabs have some very useful improvements. For example, the Vuex tab comes with the ability to directly update the state from inside DevTools. To access that functionality, simply open Chrome DevTools by pressing the *F12* key. The best way to position the DevTools to use the Vue extension is by setting it to the `Dock to bottom` option. This option is accessible by pressing the three vertical dots icon (the *Customize and control DevTools* icon), which can be found right next to the DevTools close icon in the very top-right corner of the DevTools pane.

Once you have **Dock to bottom** enabled, the **Vue** tab open, and inside it, the Vuex tab active, you will see two panes. Initially, the left pane lists **Base State**. This is the pane that lists all of the mutations and allows us to run time travel debugging. The right pane lists the actual payload, state, and mutations, so it gives us a more fine-grained view of what is happening in any given mutation. To time travel to any specific mutation, just hover over it and click the *Time Travel* icon. You also have the option of running `Commit` or `Revert` on any of the mutations listed. As you might guess, while the `Commit` command will perform a commit on the currently hovered mutation, the `Revert` command will undo the specific mutation's commit.

Another useful and interesting feature is the ability to update the state right from the Vuex tab. For example, let's say that we click the `Eat fruit!` button a few times. Now, we can click on any given `decrementCounter` mutation in the mutations pane, and we'll get the following information in the right pane:

```
▼ mutation
    payload: 1
    type: ''decrementCounter''
▼ state
    count: 1
▼ getters
    counter: 1
```

It is very simple to use this pane. If we need to updated our state, hovering over `count: 1` inside the `state` entry will trigger four icons to appear: the *Edit value* icon, the minus icon, the plus icon, and the *Copy value* icon, shown as three vertical dots. Here, we can also see the proof of `getters` being read-only. Hovering over the `getters` entry will not show any editing icons. Contrary to that, the `state` and `mutation` entries can both be edited from this pane.

Improving our fruit counter app

In this section, we will make some improvements to our fruit counter app. The goal is to see how we can go about extending our apps using Vuex.

We will update our app by adding additional functionality. Namely, we'll add buttons for different fruits: apples and pears. The number of fruits to eat and the number and kind of fruits eaten will appear in our app too.

Here is the updated JS code. We begin with defining the state in the store:

```
const store = new Vuex.Store({
  state: {
    count: 5,
    apples: 0,
    pears: 0
  },
```

Next, we set up the getters:

```
getters: {
  counter(state) {
    return state.count;
  },
```

```
      appleCount(state) {
        return state.apples;
      },
      pearCount(state) {
        return state.pears;
      }
    },
```

When defining mutations, we
need decrementWithApplesCounter and decrementWithPearsCounter, and the
resetCounter functionality:

```
    mutations: {
      decrementWithApplesCounter(state, payload) {
        state.count = state.count - 1;
        state.count < 0 ? (state.count = 0) : (state.count, state.apples
          += 1);
      },
      decrementWithPearsCounter(state, payload) {
        state.count = state.count - 1;
        state.count < 0 ? (state.count = 0) : (state.count, state.pears
          += 1);
      },
      resetCounter(state) {
        state.count = 5;
        state.apples = 0;
        state.pears = 0;
      }
    },
```

Next, we'll list our actions, decrementWithApples, decrementWithPears, and reset:

```
    actions: {
      decrementWithApples(state, payload) {
        setTimeout(() => {
          state.commit("decrementWithApplesCounter", payload);
        }, 1000)
      },
      decrementWithPears(state, payload) {
        state.commit("decrementWithPearsCounter", payload);
      },
      reset(state) {
        state.commit("resetCounter");
      }
    }
  });
```

We'll wrap it up by adding the Vue constructor:

```
const app = new Vue({
  el: "#app",
  store: store,
  computed: {
    count() {
      return store.getters.counter;
    },
    apples() {
      return store.getters.appleCount;
    },
    pears() {
      return store.getters.pearCount;
    }
  },
  methods: {
    eatApples(payload) {
      store.dispatch("decrementWithApples", payload);
    },
    eatPears(payload) {
      store.dispatch("decrementWithPears", payload);
    },
    counterReset() {
      store.dispatch("reset");
    }
  }
});
```

As we see in this code, we can update more than one variable value in a JS ternary. We are also "imitating" a call to the server with the `setTimeout()` function call; this is unnecessary, but used as an example of a more complex asynchronous operation.

The updated HTML code will look like this:

```
<div id="app" class="p-3">
  <h1>Fruit to eat: {{ count }}</h1>
  <p>Eaten: {{ apples }} apples, {{ pears }} pears</p>
  <button v-on:click="eatApples(1)" class="btn btn-success">
    An apple!
  </button>
  <button v-on:click="eatPears(1)" class="btn btn-warning">
    A pear!
  </button>
  <button v-on:click="counterReset()" class="btn btn-danger">
    Reset the counter
  </button>
</div>
```

The updated example app can be found here: `https://codepen.io/AjdinImsirovic/pen/EdNaaO`.

Summary

In this chapter, we got acquainted with Vuex, a powerful Vue plugin that helps us manage state from a centralized, global store. We learned about what state is and why we need to centralize data stores in more complex apps. We discussed unidirectional data flow and its implementation in Vuex, through the use of getters, store mutations, and store actions. We moved from theory to practice by first building a simple app, then learning how to make our development process easier with the help of the Vue Devtools extension.

In the next section, we will work with routing using Vue-router and we'll look at server-side rendering with Nuxt.

Using Nuxt.js and Vue-Router

8

With the rise of **Single-Page Applications** (**SPAs**), a number of specific issues have occurred. There have been various attempts at solving these issues, and some common solutions arose from these attempts. In this section, we will look at issues surrounding SPAs and ways of addressing and solving these issues in Vue.

In this chapter, we will work with Nuxt.js and Vue-Router to understand a number of concepts:

- Single-page applications
- Initial page load
- Server-side rendering and universal web apps
- Installing Nuxt.js
- Nuxt pages as routes
- Linking pages with the `nuxt-link` tag

We'll begin by understanding just what SPAs are and how they work.

Single-page applications and server-side rendering

Traditionally, web servers only serve static content. When a user makes a request to a link within an app, usually the server processes that request and sends the result of that processing to the client as an entire page, with HTML, CSS, and JS served by the browser. This happens when requesting each route in a web app. If a developer wants to see what was sent by the browser, it is as simple as running the `view source` command in your browser of choice.

The shortcut key for the view source command is traditionally *Ctrl + U* in some browsers, such as Chrome and Firefox.

With the push for the experience on the web to be more like what we have on desktops, we have seen the rise of SPAs in recent years. Examples of popular SPAs include Gmail, Twitter, and Google Maps.

The way that an SPA works is this: when a user navigates through different pages (routes) on a site, the browser does not download a whole new page with a whole new request to the server. Rather than downloading full pages from a server each time a user visits a route, SPAs render everything on the client. Requests to the server are made only to get new data.

A good test for deciding whether a web app can qualify as an SPA is this: does visiting a different route in the app cause the entire app to refresh? If it doesn't, then it's an SPA.

An SPA requests new data from the server while traditional web apps download entire pages from the server.

This usually means that all of the SPA code will be downloaded in one page load—the **initial page load**. This includes HTML, CSS, and JS—all the code without which an SPA would not run. The downside of this approach is that the download time can be substantial when running on slower networks or due to the sheer size of an app, especially given the fact that a lot of these SPAs are full of JavaScript code.

However, as mentioned before, the goal of SPAs is to provide an excellent user experience, to behave like desktop apps, with instant execution and without latency.

A solution to this problem was the introduction of **server-side rendering**. Server-side rendering is simply the ability of a frontend framework to prepare the HTML, CSS, and JS on the server so that, when a user visits our SPA, instead of their browser having to download the full app in one go, it only downloads a portion of this code—a fragment of the full SPA—which, regardless, still allows the user to interact with the page. Through concepts such as code splitting and rehydration, an SPA seamlessly downloads only that part of the application that is needed to start using it, and only then downloads the rest of the SPA, while the user is already interacting with it. This approach reduces the latency of the initial load.

Another major issue of SPAs in the past was the problem of not being readable by search engine crawlers. Since these crawlers cannot run JavaScript when crawling an SPA website, the visiting search engine bot would not see that SPA's content. Hence, server-side rendering is an elegant approach to both speed up a web app for the user and make it more accessible for indexing by search engine bots.

When a web app can render web pages both on the server and on the client, it is referred to as a **universal web app**. A universal web app is basically an SPA that has SSR ability.

Many modern frontend frameworks have their own SSR implementations. In Vue, this is what we call Nuxt.js.

Installing Nuxt.js and previewing the default project

To serve different routes, in the background Nuxt.js uses Vue-router. To keep things simple, we'll focus on using Nuxt.js.

There are a few ways to get started with Nuxt.js. One option is via the `vue init` command. Another one is with a practice that is common, which is the `create-nuxt-app` command, similar to `create-elm-app` or `create-react-app`.

Installing Nuxt.js with the vue init command

Let's begin by finding a location on our drive to save our new Nuxt app, and then use the `vue init` command to create it:

```
vue init nuxt-community/stater-template chapter8
```

Running this command without `vue init` being installed might return the following message in the console:

```
Command vue init requires a global addon to be installed.
Please run yarn global add @vue/cli-init and try again.
```

Hence, to rectify the issue, simply run this:

```
yarn global add @vue/cli-init
```

This will take some time, but ultimately we'll end up being able to run the **vue init** command:

```
vue init nuxt-community/starter-template chapter8
```

This time, running the preceding command will result in a few questions that we need to answer, so that the project can be configured to our liking. Similar to what we've seen with Vue-cli, to accept the defaults, we can simply press the *Enter* key.

This is the output to the console with all of the questions and answers:

```
? Project name (chapter8)
? Project name chapter8
? Project description (Nuxt.js project)
? Project description Nuxt.js project
? Author (AuthorName <author@email.com>)
? Author AuthorName <author@email.com>)
   vue-cli Generated "chapter 8"
  To get started:
    cd chapter8
    npm install # Or yarn
    npm run dev
```

Let's run these commands as described. We'll cd into the chapter8 folder, then run npm install. This will produce an output that includes some nice ASCII art of the Nuxt logo, a list of contributors and backers, and other project information. Now, we can run the npm run dev command, which will result in the following output:

```
[11:12:14] Building project
[11:12:14] Builder initialized
...
[11:12:33] Listening on http://localhost:3000
```

If we visit the page at localhost:3000, we'll be greeted with the standard welcome screen, with the Nuxt.js logo, under which there will be our project's name (**chapter8**), and two buttons: links to the documentation and to the project's GitHub repository.

Debugging an eslint error

At the time of writing of this book, even though all of the software was up to date, eslint was throwing an error. If, after running npm run dev, you would open localhost:3000, you might have seen the following error in the upper-left corner of the page that reads that the eslint module is undefined.

If this happens, you can fix it by opening the `nuxt.config.js` file inside your code editor and replacing all of the code after line 23 with this:

```
build: {
  /*
  ** Run ESLint on save
  */
  /*
  extend (config, { isDev, isClient }) {
    if (isDev && isClient) {
      config.module.rules.push({
        enforce: 'pre',
        test: /\.(js|vue)$/,
        loader: 'eslint-loader',
        exclude: /(node_modules)/
      })
    }
  }
  */
  extend(config) {
    if (process.server && process.browser) {
      config.module.rules.push({
        enforce: 'pre',
        test: /\.(js|vue)$/,
        loader: 'eslint-loader',
        exclude: /(node_modules)/
      })
    }
  }
}
```

In the preceding code, we've commented out the offending code and replaced it with the correct code, to be able to compare the differences and understand what needs fixing.

We can now rerun the `npm run dev` command and we should see the app without any errors, at `localhost:3000`.

Installing with create-nuxt-app

Alternatively, we can use the `create-nuxt-app` command. First, we'll need to install it globally, so that we can use it anywhere on our computer:

```
npm install -g create-nuxt-app
```

This command is the global install, and it might take some time. A successful installation will result in a few lines logged to console, namely the location on the local drive where `create-nuxt-app` has been installed, and some other information, similar to this:

```
+ create-nuxt-app@2.1.1
added 401 packages in 20.234s
```

Next, let's point our console to the desired folder, and then run this command:

```
create-nuxt-app chapter8b
```

Similar to the first installation approach, this one will also produce a number of questions with preset answers that we can accept by simply pressing the *Enter* key. This is the list of questions with the default answers accepted:

```
$ create-nuxt-app chapter8b
> Generating Nuxt.js project in C:\Users\PC\Desktop\chapter8b
? Project name (chapter8b)
? Project name chapter8b
? Project description (My smashing Nuxt.js project)
? Project description My smashing Nuxt.js project
? Use a custom server framework (Use arrow keys)
? Use a custom server framework none
? Use a custom UI framework (Use arrow keys)
? Use a custom UI framework none
? Choose rendering mode (Use arrow keys)
? Choose rendering mode Universal
? Use axios module (Use arrow keys)
? Use axios module no
? Use eslint (Use arrow keys)
? Use eslint no
? Use prettier (Use arrow keys)
? Use prettier no
? Author name (AuthorName)
? Author name AuthorName
? Choose a package manager (Use arrow keys)
? Choose a package manager npm
Initialized empty Git repository in C:/Users/PC/Desktop/chapter8b/.git/
```

Similar to the previous installation, we can see the instructions for running the boilerplate project, as follows:

```
To get started:

  cd chapter8b
  npm run dev

To build & start for production:
```

```
cd chapter8b
npm run build
npm start
```

So, let's run `cd chapter8b` and follow it up with `npm run dev`. The output will be almost identical to the previous installation method.

Editing the index.vue file

Let's also edit our `index.vue` file, inside the `pages` folder. This is the root route of our app. The change we'll make is minimal: we'll delete all of the code inside the `<div class="links">` tag. After the update, that snippet of code should look like this:

```
<div class="links">
  <p>Vue Quickstart is a simple introduction to Vue</p>
</div>
```

Since webpack in the background is refreshing our page, we should see the result of this change in our browser, after we save our changes:

So far, we have seen how to initialize a new Vue Nuxt project in two different ways. In the next section, we'll look at the Nuxt-flavored implementation of the `convention-over-configuration` approach: pages as routes.

Nuxt pages as routes

The *convention-over-configuration* approach was popularized by Ruby on Rails. It is an opinionated approach to web development that sets up some things in a framework in a set-and-forget manner. When we say that it is opinionated, it simply means that out of several possibilities to approach an issue, the developers of the framework chose one specific way of doing things, and that approach is the only way that something is done.

We can say that Nuxt.js is opinionated because it follows the convention of pages as routes. Thus, instead of us having to manually set up routes in our apps—that is, rather than having to *configure* them—the framework follows a simple *convention*. Inside the pages folder, the `index.vue` file acts as the root route: `/`. This means that if we run our app, visiting the root route at `localhost:3000` is equal to visiting `localhost:3000/index.vue`.

Similarly, if we create a file called `about.vue` and place it inside the pages folder, to view this file we'd need to visit the `localhost:3000/about` route.

So, let's do just that. In our pages folder, we'll make a new file and call it `contact.vue`. Inside that file, we'll add the following code:

```
<template>
  <h1>Contact</h1>
</template>
```

This is all that is needed for the `/contact` route to become available, which you can see for yourself by navigating to `localhost:3000/contact`. We can even make this file the default root route of the `contact` folder. In that case, we'd have to create a subfolder inside the `pages` folder, and give it the name of `contact`. Now, we could create an `index.vue` file inside the newly created `contact` folder, and the route will remain the same. Only our file and folder structure inside the `pages` folder has been slightly altered, but the end result is the same.

However, separating files like this into subfolders will make it easier to stay organized as you add more files.

Adding navigation to Nuxt apps via the components folder

At this point in our app development, it would be great to have the navigation in place. Navigation itself is not a page; it is a component that should exist in each page of our app. Therefore, let's create it by opening the `components` folder and adding a new file, which we'll call `Navigation.vue`. Let's add this code to it:

```html
<template>
  <div class="navigation">
    <ul>
        <li><nuxt-link to="/">Home</nuxt-link></li>
        <li><nuxt-link to="/contact">Contact</nuxt-link></li>
        <li><nuxt-link to="/news">News</nuxt-link></li>
    </ul>
  </div>
</template>

<style scoped>
.navigation {
    width: 100%;
    margin: 0;
    padding: 20px;
    background: orange;
    color: #444;
    font-family: Arial, sans-serif;
    font-size: 20px;
}
ul {
    list-style: none;
}
ul li {
    display: inline-block;
}
</style>
```

Note the `<nuxt-link>` tag. It is just a wrapper over the Vue-router implementation, and the `to="..."` attribute's value is where we specify the actual URL, which is just the name of our specific file inside the `pages` folder.

Next, let's locate the `layouts` folder, and inside of it, in the `default.vue` file, let's add the `Navigation` component inside the template, so that it looks like this:

```html
<template>
 <div>
```

```
<Navigation></Navigation>
<nuxt />
</div>
</template>
```

> Note that we can self-close components, so that instead of
> `<Navigation></Navigation>`, we could write the shorthand version,
> which is simply `<Navigation />`.

We need to make sure to import the `Navigation` component by adding the `script` tag just under the `template` tag:

```
<script>
import Navigation from '@/components/Navigation'
export default {
 components: {
 Navigation
 }
}
</script>
```

At this point, our homepage, with the navigation update, will look like this:

Now that we have our navigation in place, we'll add another page, which we'll call `News.vue`, with the following code:

```
<template>
  <h1>News</h1>
</template>
```

At this point, we have three links in our navigation, so now we can focus on adding some more content to each page.

Adding content to our Nuxt app's pages

Let's update the `News.vue` component:

```
<template>
  <section class="news">
    <h1>News</h1>
    <hr>
    <article>
        <h2>We are taking orders for our new product</h2>
        <div>
            Lorem ipsum dolor sit amet, consectetur adipisicing elit.
Laudantium perspiciatis dolorem blanditiis maxime doloremque quibusdam
obcaecati autem enim ipsum deserunt. Aliquid dolor consequatur repellendus
odit, dolores possimus ab cum et voluptatem placeat sunt perferendis porro,
eligendi perspiciatis harum pariatur veniam quo sed, reprehenderit
voluptates maiores hic! Sint, facilis voluptatibus animi!
        </div>
    </article>
    <article>
        <h2>Our website is live</h2>
        <div>
            Lorem ipsum dolor sit amet, consectetur adipisicing elit.
Delectus unde fugit quod, tempore enim obcaecati quam eius explicabo
voluptates quo consequatur! Ad iste consequuntur dolorem minima at
cupiditate veniam saepe voluptatum, qui hic corporis modi repellendus illum
natus optio aut! Omnis praesentium placeat pariatur neque dolorum eaque,
labore at et dignissimos impedit nobis, commodi rerum. Debitis est
exercitationem ipsa, commodi nihil! Inventore minus ex, quam, facilis ut
fuga unde harum possimus dolore ea voluptatum non debitis nihil ipsum
repellendus aut dolorum nam nostrum assumenda eveniet corrupti consequatur
obcaecati provident alias! Ad est minus repudiandae aliquid maxime
provident labore. Asperiores, qui!
        </div>
    </article>
  </section>
```

```
</template>

<script>

</script>

<style scoped>
    .news {
        max-width: 500px;
        margin: 0 auto;
        padding-top: 30px;
        font-size: 20px;
    }
    .news article div {
        line-height: 30px;
    }
    h1, h2 {
        padding-top: 20px;
        padding-bottom: 20px;
    }
</style>
```

The news link will now look like this:

Next, let's update the `Contact.vue` component:

```
<template>
  <section class="contact">
    <h1>Contact</h1>
    <hr>
    <article>
        <h2>Feel free to get in touch!</h2>
        <div>
            <p>Our managers:</p>
            <ul>
                <li>John Doe, +01 123 4567</li>
                <li>Jane Doe, +01 124 4567</li>
                <li>Another Person, +01 125 4567</li>
            </ul>
        </div>
    </article>
  </section>
</template>

<script>

</script>

<style scoped>
    .contact {
        max-width: 500px;
        margin: 0 auto;
        padding-top: 30px;
        font-size: 20px;
    }
    .contact article div {
        line-height: 30px;
    }
    h1, h2 {
        padding-top: 20px;
        padding-bottom: 20px;
    }
</style>
```

We will not be altering the original homepage of our Nuxt.js project. The reason for limited changes is we only need to have a few pages with some dummy content, so that we can continue to the next section, where we'll see how to add page transitions to our Nuxt.js app.

Adding page transitions to our Nuxt.js app

As we learned in Chapter 6, *Transitions and Animations*, Vue comes with a wide array of ways to add interactivity, transitions, and animations to our apps. To make this process faster, we will use animations from Animate.css, with some slight modifications.

In Nuxt, we can use page transition hooks just like we already learned. We'll simply replace the v letter inside the .v-* transition hooks with .page-*. All the functionality, and the way everything works, will stay the same.

Let's begin by opening the pages/index.vue file and adding this code at the top of its style tag:

```
.page-enter-active, .page-leave-active {
  transition: opacity 1s;
}
.page-enter, .page-leave-active {
  opacity: 0;
}
```

Next, we'll open the contact.vue file and add this code at the top of its style tag:

```
.page-enter-active {
    animation: zoomIn .5s;
}
@keyframes zoomIn {
from {
    opacity: 0;
    transform: scale3d(0.4, 0.4, 0.4);
}

50% {
    opacity: 1;
}
}

.zoomIn {
animation-name: zoomIn;
}
```

Finally, we'll update the top of the `style` tag of `news.vue` with this code:

```
.page-enter-active {
    animation: bounce .5s;
}
.page-leave-active {
    animation: bounce .5s;
}
@keyframes bounce {
    from,
    20%,
    55%,
    85%,
    to {
        animation-timing-function: cubic-bezier(0.320, 0.70, 0.355, 1);
        transform: translate3d(0, 0, 0);
    }

    40%,
    43% {
        animation-timing-function: cubic-bezier(0.700, 0.05, 0.855,
          0.06);
        transform: translate3d(0, -30px, 0);
    }

    70% {
        animation-timing-function: cubic-bezier(0.700, 0.05, 0.855,
        0.06);
        transform: translate3d(0, -15px, 0);
    }

    90% {
        transform: translate3d(0, -4px, 0);
    }
}
```

Feel free to test out your app at this point and see how you achieved a significant visual improvement with only a few changes to the `style` tags in your route files.

 In this chapter, we got acquainted with the basics of building a rudimentary Nuxt.js app. There are many ways in which this can be improved and built upon. To continue building better apps and learning more about running Vue apps on Node, feel free to refer to other titles in the Packt library, such as *Full Stack Web Development with Vue.js and Node*.

Summary

In this chapter, we learned about single-page applications, the ideas that led to their appearance, and the challenges that their implementation brings, such as issues with the initial page load. We also learned about solutions to SPA-related problems, such as server-side rendering, as well as how Nuxt.js helps us build universal web apps. We learned about installing Nuxt.js and setting up Nuxt.js pages as routes. We linked our Vue app's routing using the `nuxt-link` tag, and we added some content to each of the pages. Finally, to build up from what we learned in the previous chapters, we added some page transitions for a smoother user experience.

This brings us to the end of *Vue JS Quick Start*. We have gone through a whole array of basic Vue JS concepts. As a quick overview, we can reiterate some of the things we've covered: mustache templates, directives, modifiers, methods, computed properties, watchers, components (global and local), props, lifecycle hooks, vue-cli, slots, parent-child component communication, filters, mixins, custom directives and plugins, transitions, animations, transition components, integrating third-party animations, binding styles, working with transition groups and JavaScript animation hooks, SPAs, the concepts of state and store, one-way data flows, using Vuex, working with initial page load, Nuxt, SSR, and universal web apps.

In this short book, we have covered a lot of ground. We had to keep things basic in order to see the big picture of all the moving parts that comprise Vue JS. Where to go from here?

There are several ways in which you can build your Vue-related skills further. You could focus on understanding how to work with server-side technologies, such as Node, Laravel, or .NET Core. You could also work with VuePress—a way to built static JS-powered sites with Vue. Or you might want to check out *Vuex Quick Start Guide*.

To make it easier to continue improving your Vue.js skills, there are over two dozen titles in the Packt library at your disposal, including titles that deal with the topics listed in this summary.

Other Books You May Enjoy

If you enjoyed this book, you may be interested in these other books by Packt:

Full-Stack Vue.js 2 and Laravel 5
Anthony Gore

ISBN: 978-1-78829-958-9

- Core features of Vue.js to create sophisticated user interfaces
- Build a secure backend API with Laravel
- Learn a state-of-the-art web development workflow with Webpack
- Full-stack app design principles and best practices
- Learn to deploy a full-stack app to a cloud server and CDN
- Managing complex application state with Vuex
- Securing a web service with Laravel Passport

Vue.js 2 Design Patterns and Best Practices
Paul Halliday

ISBN: 978-1-78883-979-2

- Understand the theory and patterns of Vue.js
- Build scalable and modular Vue.js applications
- Take advantage of Vuex for reactive state management.
- Create Single Page Applications with vue-router.
- Use Nuxt for FAST server side rendered Vue applications.
- Convert your application to a Progressive Web App (PWA) and add ServiceWorkers, offline support, and more
- Build your app with Vue.js by following up with best practices and explore the common anti-patterns to avoid

Leave a review - let other readers know what you think

Please share your thoughts on this book with others by leaving a review on the site that you bought it from. If you purchased the book from Amazon, please leave us an honest review on this book's Amazon page. This is vital so that other potential readers can see and use your unbiased opinion to make purchasing decisions, we can understand what our customers think about our products, and our authors can see your feedback on the title that they have worked with Packt to create. It will only take a few minutes of your time, but is valuable to other potential customers, our authors, and Packt. Thank you!

Index